THE PARABLES OF JESUS

THE PARABLES OF JESUS

GLIMPSES OF GOD'S REIGN

Neal F. Fisher

CROSSROAD • NEW YORK

1990

The Crossroad Publishing Company
370 Lexington Avenue, New York, NY 10017

First published as *The Parables of Jesus: Glimpses of the New Age*, by
the Women's Division, Board of Global Ministries, United Methodist
Church, copyright © 1979 by Neal F. Fisher.
This revised edition copyright © 1990 by Neal F. Fisher.

Printed in the United States of America

Library of Congress Cataloging-in-Publication Data

Fisher, Neal F. (Neal Floyd), 1936-
    The parables of Jesus : glimpses of God's reign / Neal F. Fisher.
Rev. ed.
      p. cm.
    Includes bibliographical references and indexes.
    ISBN: 0-8245-1039-9
    1. Jesus Christ — Parables. 2. Bible. N.T. Gospels — Criticism,
interpretation, etc. I. Title.
BT375.2.F53   1990
226.8'06 — dc20   90-37974
                                           CIP

For Ila

Contents

Foreword to the First Edition   xi

Foreword to the Revised Edition   xiii

Introduction: Pioneers in Time   1

Part I   The Coming of God's Reign

1 Jesus and God's Reign   7
God's Reign as Crisis and Disruption   7
Expectations for the Age to Come   8
The Clash of the Old Age and the New Reign of God   11
Questions and Suggested Methods   17

2 Jesus and the Parables   20
The Importance of the Parables   20
Jesus' Style of Teaching   21
What Is a Parable?   23
Jesus' Uses of the Parables   26
Questions and Suggested Methods   31

Part II   Entering God's Reign

3 The Irruption of God's Reign   39
The Assault on Satanic Powers   40
*Parables of the House and Kingdom Divided and the
Strong Man's House*   40
The Suddenness of the Coming of God's Reign   42
The Parable of the Doorkeeper   44

The Parable of the Faithful and Wise Servant   45
The Parable of the Burglar   47
The Parable of the Fig Tree   47
The Parable of the Ten Maidens   48
Incompatibility of the New and the Old   50
*The Parables of New Patches on Old Garments and
    New Wine / New Wineskins*   50
Questions and Suggested Methods   51

4 The Joy of God's Reign   55
The Return of the Lost   58
The Parable of the Lost Sheep   58
The Parable of the Lost Coin   61
The Parable of the Prodigal Son   63
The Joy of Discovery   70
The Parables of the Hidden Treasure and of the Pearl   70
Questions and Suggested Methods   71

5 God's Reign as Reversal of Conventional Notions   76
Who Is Righteous?   78
The Parable of the Pharisee and the Publican   78
The Parable of the Two Sons   80
The Parable of the Rich Man and Lazarus   81
The Parable of the Good Samaritan   83
Astonished by Grace   86
The Parable of the Laborers in the Vineyard   86
Accumulated Wealth   89
The Parable of the Rich Fool   89
Questions and Suggested Methods   90

6 The Response Required   93
Counting the Cost   94
*The Parables of the Tower Builder and the King
    Contemplating a Campaign*   94
Taking Drastic Steps   95
The Parable of the Unjust Steward   95
The Urgency of Making a Choice   98
The Parable of the Marriage Feast   98
Showing Mercy   100
The Parable of the Unmerciful Servant   100

Surrendering Pretension 102
   The Parables of the Choice Places at Table and
     the Servant's Wages   102
Questions and Suggested Methods 104

7 Assurance of God's Reign   107
The Miracle of the Appearance of God's Reign 107
   The Parable of the Sower   108
   The Parable of the Seed Growing Secretly   113
   The Parable of the Weeds   114
   The Parable of the Mustard Seed   114
   The Parable of the Leaven   115
God's Readiness to Bring in God's Reign 116
   The Parable of the Friend at Midnight   116
   The Parable of the Unjust Judge   118
Judgment Beginning Even Now 120
   The Parable of the Closed Door   121
   The Parable of the Last Judgment   122
   The Parable of the Talents   124
   The Parables of the Barren Fig Tree and the Net   125
   The Parable of the Wicked Tenants   127
Questions and Suggested Methods 129

Part III   Living in God's Reign

8 Living in God's Reign   137
The World of the Parables and Our Own 138
   The End of an Age   138
   Focus upon the Future   141
   The Search for a Messiah   142
Parables as Alternative Futures 144
   The Shock of the Unexpected   144
   Deliverance from the Demonic   145
The Gift of a New Expectation 147
A Tangible Hope 148
The Parables as Invitations to God's Reign 150
   The Church as Parable of God's Reign   152
Questions and Suggested Methods 154

Appendix: Types of Parables in the Synoptic Gospels   157

Glossary   161

Bibliography   165

Parables in the Synoptic Gospels   168

Index of Scripture References   170

Index of Authors   175

Foreword to the First Edition

This book was prepared during the hectic months when I was making a shift from my work with the Board of Global Ministries of the United Methodist Church to teaching and administrative responsibilities at Boston University School of Theology. Associations in both communities have helped to open my eyes to the startling message of the parables. Through the Board of Global Ministries, I have met numbers of people who demonstrate their commitment to the New Age in remarkable and often heroic mission undertakings and who, without pretension, offer glimpses of its power in the affairs of individuals and communities.

New ties with students and faculty of Boston University School of Theology have likewise been instructive. Dean Richard D. Nesmith has contributed not only his early and enthusiastic support for the undertaking and periodic embarrassing inquiries about its progress; he has also helped to protect some moments in an otherwise full schedule to complete the book. Professor Howard Clark Kee has offered invaluable assistance and encouragement in several conversations related to the book, and he has contributed helpful suggestions for its improvement following a reading of it in manuscript form.

I am indebted to Dr. John J. Vincent, Director of the Urban Theological Unit in Sheffield, England, for the long conversations we have had on themes treated in this book. I have been challenged both by his perspective on the parables and the convincing manner in which he and his co-workers are embodying them in mission.

These persons have all added immeasurably to the study. The flaws that remain are the responsibility of the author and not that of those named.

Many of the considerations raised here have been subjected to the critical but friendly scrutiny of my wife, Ila, and our teenage son and daughter, Kirk and Bryn, during some summer weeks when the first draft was written. Each has patiently helped in important ways. Most of all I wish to express my gratitude to Ila for her winsome loyalty to the New Age and for the concrete ways in which she points to its appearing.

Foreword to the Revised Edition

Preparation of a revised edition of this book on the parables of Jesus provides a welcome opportunity to augment the treatment of some topics and to draw upon studies of the subject that have appeared after publication of the first edition.

The aim in this edition, as it was in the first edition, is to consider the parables in the first three Gospels and to arrange them according to recurring themes in Jesus' proclamation of the Reign of God. Care has been taken to understand how and why Jesus typically spoke in parables and to hear them as closely as possible to the way they would have been heard and appropriated by his contemporaries.

A number of recent studies of the parables have centered upon the formal structures to be found in parables as literary creations and the relationship of the parables to other literary forms in Jesus' time and our own. These purely literary questions, while they have their own importance and merit, are not a part of the central aim of this study. They have been alluded to only when they have direct bearing upon that aim. Some of the more prominent writings on this subject are referred to in the notes and the bibliography.

The author is indebted to the Board of Trustees of Garrett-Evangelical Theological Seminary for offering a study leave when this revision and other projects could be undertaken and to the faculty and staff of the seminary for their generous interest and support. Special thanks are due to Mrs. Dorothy Bon-Durant, who cared so well for administrative matters during my absence and to Mrs. Frances Shuford for her expert assistance in the preparation of the manuscript. The book is inscribed to Ila, beloved partner in life and ministry.

The author is grateful for the many generous indications from readers of the first edition that the book was of benefit in studying the message of Jesus. The revised edition is offered in the hope that it may be useful to yet others in hearing and appropriating the Good News of God's Reign.

Introduction

Pioneers in Time

Many people today experience the times in which they are living as strange and alien. So much change has taken place that they feel they are in a different world. We have all, to some extent, become "pioneers in time."[1] So little of our past has prepared us to comprehend our present or our future. In other eras, people could reckon with the future by remembering their past. They knew what their grandchildren would face by recollecting their own stages in life. Now we can scarcely guess the kind of world in which our children will spend their lives — let alone that of our grandchildren. Margaret Mead has reminded us that while parents could once say, "I've been young," now their children can respond, "You never have been young in the world I am young in, and you never can be."[2]

The future confronts us not only as a place of hope and fulfillment, but also of apprehension and threat. In our more optimistic moments, we imagine that all that is awry in the present will be resolved in the future. We use such expressions as, "Some day they'll find a cure," or "It's going to take a lot of education." We assume that improved technology or information will resolve the problems that beset us.

But some of our casual expressions about the future are less hopeful. We often wonder out loud, "What is this world coming to?" or "Where is it all leading us?" In these moments, the future seems precarious at best. It looms as that distant point when all our present forebodings about war, environmental collapse, massive starvation or exhaustion of natural resources become overwhelming threats.

Experiences such as these have contributed to many persons' sense that we are living at the intersection of two epochs in human history. Whether this change is greeted with joy or viewed with alarm, voices from many quarters are telling us what we already know inwardly — that we are experiencing a significant transition.

In the sense that we have some general feeling of imminent change, we can share the mood of many who first heard Jesus. These people felt that they were living at the end of an age. They looked forward eagerly to the end of this present period of time and the beginning of the "Age to Come," when the blessings now denied would be assured. They could find neither hope nor consolation in the way things were. They lived in anticipation of the newness that God was bringing to pass; they were pioneers in time.

Christians in the centuries that have followed have, in some sense, styled themselves as pioneers in time. For one of the most basic Christian declarations is that the Reign of God, the Age to Come, has dawned in the person of Jesus, who is Messiah, or Christ. By numbering our years from the date of his birth, we show that every year before and after Christ has significance in relationship to that event. Every moment in time, according to our confession, is related to this midpoint of history.[3]

Obviously, God's purposes have not prevailed in our time. The suffering exacted from some by the greed of others has not diminished. But in the life, death, and resurrection of Jesus Christ, we have glimpsed the Age to Come. We live, therefore, as ones who are lured on through history by the hope that we find in Christ. We are confident, even in the midst of difficulty, for we have both a vision of the Age to Come and assurance in its coming: "The hope of the final victory is so much the more vivid because of the unshakably firm conviction that the battle that decides the victory has already taken place."[4]

The words of Alfred North Whitehead in describing religion, words to which we shall return at the end of this study, sketch the tone of expectancy that is appropriate in studying the New Testament, especially the parables. Religion, says Whitehead "is the vision of something which stands beyond, behind, and within, the passing flux of immediate things, something which is real, and yet waiting to be realized, something which is a remote possibility and yet the greatest of present facts, something whose possession is the final good, and yet is beyond reach: something which is the ultimate ideal and the hopeless quest."[5]

The parables allude to the Age to Come that is a happening that forever eludes us and yet is near at hand. They unveil a future that already is making an impact upon the present. Rather than listing a set of moral precepts, the parables yield a glimpse of an age in which an entirely new stance is appropriate. Just as a natural disaster, a wedding, a funeral, or a war requires distinctive behavior, so the parables set forth the context of the Reign of God that authorizes a whole new approach to life. The parables do not detail what we are to do; they suggest what is possible and fitting now that God has acted decisively in history and the powers of Satan, though still amply in evidence, are in principle undone.

In this study, we shall look at the parables first to discover as nearly as we can what Jesus actually said and meant when he spoke to his first hearers. We shall also look at what these parables reveal in us. In other words, we shall seek both to interpret the parables and allow them to interpret us.

As in any Bible study, the words of introduction and comment are intended to introduce us to the Bible itself and to the one to whom the Bible bears witness. It is assumed throughout, therefore, that the reader will have a modern translation of the Bible in hand as she or he reads the text. A synopsis of the first three Gospels, such as *Gospel Parallels*,[6] which prints Matthew, Mark, and Luke in parallel columns will be very helpful. Those interested in comparing the parables in the first three Gospels of the New Testament with other ancient manuscripts, including non-canonical gospels such as the Gospel of Thomas, will find a useful source in John Dominic Crossan's *Sayings Parallels: A Workbook for the Jesus Tradition*.[7]

As an aid in referring to the parables, a chart at the back of the book lists them as they appear in the first three Gospels and lists as well the section in *Gospel Parallels* where they may be found. The reader is encouraged to read the parables in more than one translation.

Notes

1. This phrase is suggested in a passage by Margaret Mead: "In this sense, then, of having moved into a present for which none of us was prepared by our understanding of the past, our interpretations of ongoing experience or our expectations about the future, all of us who grew up before World War II are pioneers, immigrants in time who have left behind our familiar worlds to live in a new age under conditions that are different from any we have known" (from *Culture and Commitment* [Garden City, N.Y.: Doubleday, 1970], p. 74).

2. Ibid., p. 63.

3. Oscar Cullmann, *Christ and Time*, trans. Floyd V. Filson, rev. ed. (London: SCM, 1962), pp. 19ff.

4. Ibid., p. 87. Original in italics.

5. *Science and the Modern World*, p. 228 (1933 ed.). Quoted in Ian T. Ramsey, *Christian Discourse* (London: Oxford University Press, 1965), p. 66.

6. Burton H. Throckmorton, Jr., ed., *Gospel Parallels* (New York: Thomas Nelson, 1957).

7. Philadelphia: Fortress Press, 1986. For a helpful compilation of other writings from New Testament times that help to understand the context for the Gospels, see *Documents for the Study of the Gospels*, ed. and trans. David R. Carlidge and David L. Dugan (Philadelphia: Fortress Press, 1980).

Part I

The Coming
of God's Reign

Chapter 1

Jesus and God's Reign

GOD'S REIGN AS CRISIS AND DISRUPTION

The pages of the New Testament are crackling with the mood of crisis and urgency. Jesus appears on the scene with the stark declaration:

> The time is fulfilled, and the kingdom of God is at hand; repent and believe in the gospel. (Mark 1:15; Matt. 4:17b)

No sooner has he made this announcement than he abruptly calls the fishermen Simon and Andrew and enlists them in his mission. They abandon their father, along with employees, boats, and nets, in order to join Jesus (Mark 1:16–20). Mark uses the word for "immediately" or "directly" forty-one times to describe Jesus' movements.

Jesus moves from place to place quickly, sometimes having to flee for his life from the hands of those who are outraged by his brash appeal (Luke 4:29). No sooner has Jesus begun preaching than he redefines the Law, heightening its demands (Matt. 5:20–48). The most scrupulously religious he calls hypocrites. Something definitively new is happening, he tells them; God's Reign is breaking in. Some, says Jesus, are quite capable of scanning the clouds and predicting the coming of rain, and others can foretell the onslaught of searing heat by the feel of the wind. But they, having mastered these details of daily discernment, have no idea of the nature of the times in which they

7

live. Knowing and interpreting the times become the keys to understanding the crisis that is at hand and the nature of the decision at hand (Luke 12:54–56).

As if to underline the critical nature of the times and the urgency of spreading the word, Jesus instructs the disciples to move out with dispatch. They are not to waste their time; they are not even to take the time to greet other travelers along the road (Luke 10:4), nor are they to tarry at a place in which they are not readily received (Luke 9:5). When Elijah called Elisha to follow him, he permitted him time to say good-bye to his mother and father (1 Kings 19:20); Jesus will not allow that of his disciples (Luke 9:61–62). Indeed, even the sacred obligation of mourning for six days upon the death of a parent is denied them because of the urgency of God's Reign. The dead will have to bury their own dead (Luke 9:60)!

It is in the crush of this urgent, critical situation that Jesus used parables. The nature of the events that were taking place in his ministry precluded long discourses. He employed figures of speech, quick comparisons, sharp warnings, and parables to help his hearers picture the reality of God's Reign breaking in upon them. There was not time to tarry for long discussion. The Reign of God, so ardently sought and fondly hoped for, was now breaking in, calling for decision and action. "The kingdom of God is at hand!" (Mark 1:15). In speaking thus of the Kingdom of God, Jesus was addressing in new ways hopes and expectations that had long been a part of the faith of Israel.

EXPECTATIONS FOR THE AGE TO COME

The people of Israel in the time of Jesus longed for the day when God would intervene — directly or through a divinely appointed agent — and establish the Divine Rule on earth. Some understood this divine intervention in secular terms, terms derived principally from the most illustrious of Israel's kings, David. Since the mark of kingship was to be anointed, they spoke of the agent of God's coming Reign as "the anointed one," or Messiah. The word "Messiah" was translated into Greek as *Christos* (Christ). It was the Messiah who would come to establish the Reign of God. He would gather the tribes of Israel together and from Jerusalem would establish a worldwide kingdom. Under the united rule of the Messiah, Israel would be exalted among the nations. The rule of Rome would be thrown off, and those exiled from the land would be gathered in.[1]

But a second form of hope for the Messiah also flourished in the time of Jesus. This hope, nourished among the poor and pietistic communities, such as the Essenes and Qumran on the Dead Sea, centered not upon a secular kingdom but upon a divine Reign of God. As the times worsened for Israel, those who shared this hope found it impossible to believe that God's Reign could be expressed through existing structures. They looked, therefore, for the end of this age, the epoch that was passing away, and the creation by God of the Age to Come. This coming new order was to be God's doing and God's alone. These groups believed it would be given birth in the midst of great pain and suffering and judgment upon the godless.[2] But, fearful as the sufferings preceding God's Reign were to be, God's Reign itself offered hope and blessing for the faithful who devoutly prepared for it and with penitence were ready for its appearing. These groups referred to this new world as the Kingdom of God, the Reign of God, or simply as the Age to Come. Whatever the term used, it referred to the sovereign action of God by which the Divine Rule was established and assured as the guiding principle for all.[3]

At times in Israel's history, there were those who believed that they had been given particular revelation of the end-time and recorded their revelations or visions in graphic terms. Their writings were called apocalyptic, meaning "uncovering" or "revealed." In some of the apocalyptic writings, the Reign of God was pictured coming not through the intervention of a secular Messiah but through a heavenly figure. On behalf of God, this figure would subdue all the hostile powers and bring all the nations under the Reign of God. The Hebrew word used to refer to this agent originally meant simply "a man." It is used in Daniel's vision:

> I saw in the night visions,
> and behold, with the clouds of heaven
> there came one like a son of man. (Dan. 7:13)[4]

For some, the development of belief in the Son of Man as a heavenly figure was accompanied by a belief in resurrection. In the oldest portions of Judaism, there was no belief in life after death. Many, on that account, believed that only those actually alive at the time the Messiah appeared would find the fulfillment of God's Reign. By the time of Jesus, however, many had come to believe in the resurrection. They believed that the faithful of all the past generations therefore could taste the transformation wrought by the coming of God's Reign.[5]

All these hopes and expectations were a part of the situation in which Jesus began his ministry. The terms, "Messiah" and "Son of Man" were in use in Jesus' day, though with meanings that continued to develop as the notions of the Reign of God itself developed. In the Similitudes of Enoch, the Messiah, or Christ, was identified with the apocalyptic Son of Man. But there is no assurance that Jesus' contemporaries used the two terms interchangeably.[6] What is assured is that, in the usage of Jesus and in the witnessing of the early Christian church, both Son of Man and Christ came to mean something distinctive that was not reducible to their earlier forms.

Certain images readily conveyed the hopes for the Reign of God by the people. God would rule as King (Micah 2:12ff.; 4:1–7; Isa. 24:21–23; 33:22, Zeph. 3:14–20). The people of the earth would be gathered at a great banquet presided over by God's Messiah. They frequently spoke of the Reign of God as a time of harvest and of wine. Again, it was compared to a great marriage feast. Often the figure of Elijah was prominently associated with the coming of the Messiah. It is no surprise, then, that John the Baptist was described in terms identical with those used to describe Elijah (cf. Mark 1:6 and 2 Kings 1:8). Similarly, it is not unexpected that the name of Elijah should be mentioned at several critical junctures in Jesus' ministry (Mark 8:28, 9:11, and 15:35).

Whatever form that the expectation took, there was the assurance on the part of many that God's Reign would involve fearful signs and suffering. It would be a time of judgment when those who were faithful would be separated from the unrighteous. Before the bliss of God's Reign could come in force, the righteous and the sinners alike would be subject to testing and judgment.

At the time of Jesus, great numbers of people believed that they were living in the last days of the old age. They looked confidently for the appearance of the Messiah. Messianic movements flamed forth from place to place under charismatic leaders and were then promptly snuffed out by the colonial rule of Rome. It was probably not unprecedented for a messianic leader to march at the head of his supporters into the city of Jerusalem, for it was an element of the Messiah's vocation to claim the city in the name of the Lord.

This earnest searching for the Lord's Messiah was written deeply into the devotion of the people. Many righteous people such as Simeon clung to their hope for the deliverance of Israel (Luke 2:25). In the synagogues the people regularly prayed the Kaddish:

> Magnified and sanctified be his great name in the world which he has created according to his will. May he establish his kingdom in your days and in the lifetime of all the house of Israel even speedily and at a near time.[7]

Jesus, as a regular participant in the worship of the synagogue, would have been familiar with this prayer. Indeed, the close parallels between this prayer and the petitions of the prayer that he taught his disciples ("Hallowed be thy name, thy kingdom come..."[8]) make it clear that the hope for God's coming Reign is a central focus for his ministry.

Since these expectations were a part of the thinking of the people, the appearance of John the Baptist and his announcement of the coming of God's Reign placed those who heard him on notice that the One who had been promised was soon to come.

THE CLASH OF THE OLD AGE AND
THE NEW REIGN OF GOD

The ringing declaration of the Gospel writers is that the Reign of God has arrived in the person and deeds of Jesus Christ. They had felt the force of that reign through the claim that Christ had made upon their life. They testified that, with his coming, the last decisive engagement of God against the forces of Satan had begun. God had defeated the forces of sin and death in principle through Christ, and this victory soon would become evident to all when Christ came to rule in power. When Jesus did thus return, the victory over sin and death that was already experienced in faith would become an accomplished fact for all.

Because of Christ's victory, the writers of the Gospels believed that the Reign of God inaugurated with him could be experienced now. Even while the old era exerted its power, the force of the new Reign of God could be felt. God's Reign flashed forth in sudden, unexpected ways. It was known in momentary happenings. But those who believed in Christ could experience it as a force that rocked their whole world. As they cast their full trust and reliance upon God's Reign, they lived within its power even while they found themselves among the structures of the old and fading era.

The evangelists portray Jesus' ministry, therefore, as the point of confrontation between two ages or two realms. Mark, with characteristic briskness, established in the first fifteen verses of his Gospel that God has triumphed, that Jesus is God's agent in establishing God's Reign, and that all his hearers and readers may join in the Reign of God through repentance and faith.[9] Mark announces that the Reign of God is dawning as he notes the astonishment of the people at the style of Jesus' teaching (Mark 1:22) and discloses the imminent defeat of Satan's forces by the plaintive question that the unclean spirits put to Jesus: "Have you come to destroy us?" (Mark 1:24). There is no question but that the reader is expected to answer instinctively in the affirmative.

Many of Jesus' contemporaries referred to this future state of blessing as the "Age to Come." Jesus, by contrast, employed the term "the Kingdom of God" to designate both God's intervention in human affairs and the new life obtained for the redeemed through Jesus' gracious action.[10] Today these terms do not always adequately represent the reality that was central to Jesus' ministry and the parables. In our language, "Kingdom," in addition to its sexist overtones, fails to connote the dynamic nature of the new era that Jesus announced and at once embodied. We tend to think of a geographical space or a political organization. This concept of Jesus needs to be understood not as a static entity but as a happening, an occurrence in which God's sovereign activity is made evident. Throughout the New Testament it stands for a function, for operative power, for a signal deed that discloses God's rule.[11] Mindful of this meaning, Perrin suggests English-speaking students of the New Testament might speak of the "ruling of God."[12]

It is a matter of some importance that we choose our terms wisely in speaking of this central theme in Jesus' teaching and preaching. Care is required that we as closely as possible choose words without overtones or connotations that twist and distort our understanding of Jesus' teaching.

In some ways terms such as "the New Age" or "God's New Age" might serve us well as synonyms for "the Kingdom of God." The idea of an "age" is an important one in the New Testament. It has to be translated in a variety of ways in order to communicate its meaning in English. One Greek word, *aion*, is used in the New Testament to refer to the past (Luke 1:70), the future (Matt. 12:32), the world or the universe, or the present age (Matt. 13:22 — translated as "the world"). The word suggests a way of organizing and understanding the world and its history in major blocks of time — extending from the Creation to the furthest reaches of the future.

In our normal conversation, the word "age" is used to communicate an expanse of time characterized or understood through certain key happenings or developments. We speak, for example, of the atomic age, the scientific age, the Age of Reason, or even — in the 1960s — the Age of Aquarius. An electronics store advertises its wares by a sign announcing, "The Age of the Computer is Here!" All these uses of the word "age" suggest the notion of a major period of time that bears the stamp of and is to be understood through the impact of some central event or development.

Similarly, in the New Testament, the word *aion* designates a block of time. Certain events typify or lend their name to blocks of time. In its widest scope, all the time before the coming of God's Messiah was characterized by the initial disobedience of Adam that stood at its beginning. With Christ's coming, God's New Age begins. It is characterized by Jesus' subjection of the evil powers that, until that time, had held sway.[13] Such a realm is an expanse of time and a view of the world shaped by the determinative acts of Jesus Christ that mark its advent.

The Gospel writers picture Jesus' coming as a time in which the two ages confront one another. The old age was marked by evil, sin, and disease. But within that very age they also witnessed the promise of another age. The time of blessing inaugurated in Jesus' ministry was marked by the healing of the sick, the restoration of sight to the blind, and the recovery of hearing for the deaf. Those who were in chains now were set free. The Reign of God that he embodied was a dramatic reversal of all that distorted and oppressed in the old order.

The time of fulfillment irrupted in events that flashed before people. It was never a captured or "domesticated" fact. It was always provisional and precarious. Even when Jesus said to the Seventy that he witnessed Satan falling from heaven (Luke 10:18), it was clear that the power of Satan was nonetheless not completely subdued. They struggled with it still. God's Reign was experienced in provisional appearances, sudden glimpses, recurring intimations, but never as observable, commonplace fact. Whenever it was present, apprehension of that reality depended as much upon the eyes to see and ears to hear as it did on observable facts. Jesus even called it a "secret" that many would see but not perceive and hear but not understand (Mark 4:11f.).

Sometimes we speak of two persons living in "two different worlds" or refer to a person particularly out of touch with the times as "living in a different age." Our use of the "worlds" or "age" has in that instance a kinetic feel; it suggests movement. This sense of motion may help us to grasp how the New Testament writers could hold that, even while the old order was passing through its final times, it was possible for those who cast their full reliance upon the action of God in Jesus Christ to enter into God's New Age. The old was still in force, but the new was even then in its formative stage. Until that new order, the Reign of God, was fully consummated, they would experience God's Reign in conflict with the old. That conflict between the old and the new forms the context for Jesus' ministry, including his teaching in parables.

It is apparent in this discussion of Jesus' preaching of the kingdom that no one word or phrase in our language is completely adequate for communicating what Jesus meant by the term and for avoiding confusing or misleading connotations. In an earlier edition of this study, we proposed "New Age" as such a suitable term. This phrase, however, has come to be associated in the minds of many with a certain view of personal and social change that, whatever its merit, should not be confused with Jesus' preaching of the kingdom.[14]

Concern, therefore, to find terms that preserve the kinetic quality of "kingdom" without "importing" misleading associations has prompted us in this study to refer frequently to the Kingdom of God simply as "God's Reign" or "the Reign of God." We wish by that to make it clear that the hoped-for blessing coming in Jesus' ministry is not a static state but an occurrence or happening in which God's rule is made manifest. We use these terms as the equivalents of "the Kingdom of God" or "God's New Age."

The clash between God's Reign and the existing order is nowhere more evident than in the conflict between Jesus and the religious community. Each segment of the religious community had its own world of understanding. That is, each religious community had its own implicit estimate of the historical situation, the future ahead of it, and the consequent will of God for it. Those who saw in Jesus the irruption of God's Reign were, on that account, singularly prepared to conduct themselves differently from those who rested comfortably with all the assumptions and prevailing practices of the old order.

It was, in fact, some of the most conscientiously religious people who were offended by Jesus on the grounds of religious principle. The Pharisees conscientiously and scrupulously sought to obey the full requirements of God as given to them in the Law. For them this required strict separation of the righteous from the sinners. While sometimes given to smugness about their own spiritual condition, they nonetheless viewed the Law as a gift of God given out of divine mercy for them. We have no reason to doubt the sincerity of the Pharisee in the Temple who offered thanks to God that he had not merely met the minimum requirements of the Law but had in fact exceeded them (Luke 18:9–14). This was a part of the world or realm in which he lived his life.

In any epoch there are those who benefit from the way things are and adopt the prevailing preconceptions and values as their

orientation in life. They absorb the values around them that become their world. Our values and assumptions are notable for
their ability to reinforce us and to serve our interests. People
tend to believe that they have earned their privileges, and they
believe the same will be forthcoming to anyone else who strug-
gles for them with equal diligence. This belief helps hold their
world together.

Jesus' contemporaries had a neat definition for each person.
Was a person handicapped? Then someone had sinned, and the
handicap was retribution for the sin (see the story of the man
born blind in John 9:2ff.). Was a person from another nation
or section of the country? There were reasons why that person
should be excluded or avoided (the Samaritans, for example).
Everyone was "typed" or neatly categorized into a special place.
Those categories and one's security with them in part consti-
tuted a view of the world.

Jesus represented the dissolution of a world to persons comfortable and secure in this world. The conventional assumptions
and prevailing views that provided security for them were subjected to radical question. Jesus said that those thought to be
excluded were at that very moment welcomed into the family of God. They were to inherit the Reign of God. He told
those who thought that they had established themselves in God's
favor that they would follow the prostitutes and the tax collectors into that Reign! All the care given to their religious
observance now seemed to matter little. Those who believed
that the matter of religious observance was an important test
and that they had met it were seldom able to cast their lives
in repentance and faith upon the powers and promise of God's
Reign.

But to others, the Reign of God was good news. It was a new
world for those for whom the old age offered little consolation
or hope. They had little interest in preserving the old age since,
in it, they could never hope to find vindication and blessing.
But according to Jesus, the ones who are pronounced blessed
and inherit God's Reign are the very ones who have little standing in the present order of things, those "who are driven to the
very end of the world and its possibilities." They are "the poor,
who do not fit in to the structure of the world and therefore are
rejected by the world; the mourner, for whom the world holds

no consolation; the humble, who no longer extract recognition from the world; the hungry and thirsty, who cannot live without the righteousness that God alone can promise and provide in this world."[15]

Thus, both for the well-established and the poor, the coming of Jesus represented the end of an order, the fracturing of a world. The Pharisees and scribes saw that their role as the guardians of the tradition was ended. Others, thought to be nobodies, were invited to become table companions and friends with Jesus. The world neatly established by the Law now had no clear future. The iron predictability of everyone's world was undone. Each person was faced with a new possibility in the present.

The Reign of God is like the experience of a person walking on a dark deserted road who suddenly glimpses the otherwise obscure surroundings in a flash of lightning. In an instant the countryside is suddenly splashed with light; everything comes into view. The image of the surroundings is seared upon the mind. Because of that glimpse, the person who continues walking through the darkness knows of the reality that lies behind and ahead.

The message of the New Testament is that the time through which we pass has been fractured by light. Even as we live among the marks of the old order, there are glimpses here and there of God's Reign breaking in. The two realms are in conflict. In Jesus Christ the Reign of God is present. It is this Reign glimpsed through the parables of Jesus that we are to study.

QUESTIONS AND SUGGESTED METHODS

1. What evidences do you see that we are experiencing the end of one "world" or realm and the beginning of another? Make a parallel list of the marks of the age that is ending and the marks of the new epoch that seems to be taking shape. Which marks of the new order are promising? Which are threatening?

2. The "good news" of the Gospel was heard as a promise to some and as a threat to others. Those who heard the parables first found themselves judged or affirmed in the stories they heard. Compose an interpretation of each of the following headlines that will illustrate an interpretation of the headline as promise or as threat:

- "Nations Exporting Raw Materials to U.S. Unite to Demand Fair Price"

- "Contributions to Churches No Longer Deductible in I.R.S. Code"

- "U.S.-Soviet Arms Reduction Plan Ratified in Senate"

- "Ghetto Youth to Get Preference in Municipal Jobs"

3. Hopes for the future have sometimes been used as a means of avoiding the pain of the present. Yet Jesus announced the Reign of God both as a present reality and as a hope for a future that God would bring to completion. List as many visions of the future as you see reflected in religious, political, economic, educational, and other discussions. Which of them detract the attention of people from the present? Which increase the likelihood of change in the present?

4. Prepare a list of charges that could have been (and perhaps were) leveled against Jesus labeling him as irreligious. How would those charges be phrased today in your own congregation? Which would be most serious?

5. Those who were "sinners" and tax collectors were offensive to people in Jesus' day. They often equated poverty and sickness with sinfulness. Do you detect any tendencies today to identify those who are poor also as sinners? Is poverty or racial prejudice blamed upon an alleged moral defect of those who are the victims of prejudice?

6. Nearly every time has images and symbols of a "good time coming," the time when all one's hopes and dreams will supposedly be achieved. This time is portrayed in a wide variety of ways in media, advertising, politics, religion, education, and other aspects of life today. Some in the group might clip advertisements from popular magazines and display them in a collage as a way of reminding other members of the group of popular views of the future. Others might list political slogans from recent political campaigns that convey a picture of the future.

Notes

1. Rudolf Bultmann, *Jesus and the Word*, trans. Louise Pettibone Smith and Erminie Huntress Lantero (New York: Charles Scribner's Sons, 1958), p. 41. See also Ernst Benz, *Evolution and Christian Hope*, trans. Heinz G. Frank (Garden City, N.Y.: Doubleday, 1966), pp. 1–2.

2. Benz, *Evolution and Christian Hope*, pp. 3–4.

3. D. E. Nineham, *The Gospel of St. Mark* (Baltimore: Penguin Books), p. 44.

4. Later the simile ("one like a son of man") became a title and referred to an individual rather than the redemptive community.

5. Benz, *Evolution and Christian Hope*, pp. 4–5.

6. Alan Richardson, *An Introduction to the Theology of the New Testament* (New York: Harper & Brothers, 1958), pp. 130–131.

7. Translated and quoted by Norman Perrin in his *Rediscovering the Teaching of Jesus* (New York: Harper & Row, 1976), p. 57.

8. Ibid.

9. See this emphasis in Howard Clark Kee, *Community of the New Age* (Philadelphia: Westminster, 1977), pp. 74–75.

10. Perrin, *Rediscovering the Teaching of Jesus*, pp. 59ff.

11. R. Schnackenburg, *God's Rule and Kingdom*, trans. John Murray (New York: Herder and Herder, 1963), p. 13. Quoted in Perrin, *Rediscovering the Teaching of Jesus*, p. 55.

12. Perrin, *Rediscovering the Teaching of Jesus*, p. 55.

13. See Oscar Cullmann's discussion of *aion* in *Christ and Time*, pp. 45–50, esp. p. 47.

14. For example, one best-selling book (referred to on its cover as a "New Age watershed classic") is Marilyn Ferguson's *The Aquarian Conspiracy: Personal and Social Transformation in the 1980s* (New York: St. Martin's Press [1980], 1987). See references below, chapter 8, p. 139. The book includes an extensive listing of organizations and publications affiliated in some way with the perspective of the book. One publication explicitly directing itself to the "new age" is the bi-monthly *New Age Journal*, devoted to "exploring the new frontiers of human potential." The magazine contains articles and advertisements relating to a wide array of topics, including meditation, self-improvement methods, proper diet, ecology, stress-reduction, and other similar concerns (published by Rising Star Associates, Ltd., 342 Western Avenue, Brighton, MA 02135).

15. Gunther Bornkamm, *Jesus of Nazareth*, trans. Irene and Fraser McLuskey with James M. Robinson (New York: Harper & Row, 1960), p. 76.

Chapter 2

Jesus and the Parables

THE IMPORTANCE OF THE PARABLES

The parables stand before us as literary creations to be understood in their own right. But when we study the parables, we are also looking into the most revealing apertures into Jesus' teaching and person. In the parables, it is not so much that we are instructed *by* Jesus but that we stand *with* him and view life through his eyes, learning to grasp all of life in the light of God's Reign. When we study the parables, we are not told what we must see there. Rather, the scene is set in sparse terms and we are invited to view what is before us.

The parables are particularly reliable guides, first of all, because of the soundness of the tradition by which they come to us. Stories by nature are more easily remembered than abstract statements. Vivid pictures leave memorable impressions that can be recalled long after the words of more abstract teachings have fled. Of all of the collections of traditions from Jesus' teachings that were available to the Gospel writers, the parables were probably the closest to Jesus' original words.

The language used by Jesus in the parables is specific and concrete. He spoke of a farmer sowing seed on different types of soil, of a wily manager rushing out to get allies among his townspeople before it was known that he had been fired from his job, of a man hiring help at the place in the town where the unemployed gathered waiting for someone to hire them, and of a member of an outcast group, a Samaritan, proving to be the one who was a model of a neighbor. Each story was told with just enough detail to help the hearer enter into the situation without any distracting or extraneous facts to clutter or divert.

The New Testament scholar Amos Wilder has commented at this point that what is distinctive in the parables of Jesus is "the way in which those deeper dimensions [the perspective of God's judgment and love] are married to such ordinariness and secularity." What we have in the sayings of Jesus, says Wilder, is "the counterpart of his own person and presence among men: not as a philosopher, priest, or scribe, but as an artisan; not in the desert or in the temple, but in the marketplace."[1]

The parables are allotted one-third of the space given to all Jesus' recorded teachings. The parabolic teachings, as compared to the non-parabolic, constitute the following percentages of the Gospel teachings of Jesus reported in the first three Gospels — Mark, 16 percent; Matthew, 43 percent; and Luke, 52 percent.[2] The first three Gospels record Jesus' parables. In the Gospel of John, the parables are replaced by longer allegorical interpretations of Jesus' identity and mission (such as Living Water: 4:13–15; Bread of Life: 6:35–41; Light of the World: 8:13–18; and the Door: 10:7–18; etc.).

According to the evangelists, the parables were Jesus' characteristic form of teaching. Mark went so far as to say that Jesus did not say anything to the crowds without a parable (4:34). It was doubtless his selection of incidents from daily life memorably told that moved his hearers to comment about his teaching with authority, rather than as one of the scribes (Mark 1:22).[3]

JESUS' STYLE OF TEACHING

The contrast between Jesus' teaching and that of the scribes was astonishing to his hearers, as Mark reported. The scribes taught in scholarly exposition on the Scriptures, citing the opinions of earlier commentators and focusing upon subtle shadings of meaning. Jesus frequently referred to the Scriptures in his teaching and conversation, but his teaching was not about religion conventionally understood. He talked about the common experience of people as they watched the miracle of growth from a seed to a tree, as they observed the behavior of faithful and unfaithful sons, or as they tried to sew patches on old garments. These experiences became points of comparison by which Jesus announced the reality of the Reign of God breaking in — the time of salvation that they could enter even then.

Characteristically, Jesus' style was to turn a question upon the questioner. A lawyer asked him his legal definition of a neighbor. Jesus answered by telling him a story and putting a sharper question to the lawyer: Who acted as a neighbor to a man robbed, beaten, and deserted on a desolate road? He taught thus by telling parables.

In drawing upon parables as a major teaching vehicle, Jesus was not utilizing a unique form. Parables were used by rabbis who were his contemporaries.[4] At least nine parables can be identified in the Hebrew Bible; the most famous is Nathan's story of the ewe lamb (2 Sam. 12:1–4).[5] Other examples may be found in Isaiah 5:1–7, 1 Kings 20:35–40, and Ezekiel 19:2–9.[6]

Many of the parables used by rabbis in Jesus' time center on themes that Jesus also used, such as the action of a king, the giving of a feast, or the planting of a field. Yet Jesus' use of parables was distinctive. The rabbis used parables to explain the otherwise hidden meaning of a passage of Scripture or to trap an adversary in an argument.[7] They used parables to illustrate or clarify a point that could have been summarized without such a figure of speech. The parables were explicitly linked to a Scriptural text or a concrete moral situation and taught by example and detailed allegorical comparisons. Jesus, on the other hand, did not use parables to explain an authoritative text: "The parables [of Jesus] are the preaching itself and are not merely serving the purpose of a lesson that is quite independent of them."[8] Jesus taught not merely to convey information but to effect a transformation in the hearer.[9] Jesus let the story speak for itself, inviting the hearer to participate in it and to take a stand. The topics, drawn as they were from life as people lived it, did not require extensive elaboration.

Jesus taught that the Reign of God of which he was bearer and agent was to be glimpsed in actions and relationships that people experienced day by day. Jesus told people that they were dealing with issues of God's Reign right in the midst of their secular affairs.[10] God's Reign was breaking in all around them. And, in the stories of the everyday, there were glimpses of what this new era of salvation was all about. If they could put themselves into a good story, they would have an opportunity to experience God's Reign in miniature. By its very nature, God's Reign was not a place or a time so much as it was a happening that was a gift of God. The ultimate, said Jesus, was to be found in the immediate.

WHAT IS A PARABLE?

Parables, then, were central in Jesus' teaching. We now turn our attention to the nature of parables themselves. Many of us first heard a parable described as "an earthly story with a heavenly meaning." That is partly true, yet it does some disservice in suggesting that the parables discuss common topics for the sole purpose of disclosing something about heaven that could be told in quite other words. The parable actually uses an earthly story to reveal a reality that is breaking in upon human experience. The story is told not to divert us from life but rather to disclose to us, as we participate in the parable, the nature of God's Reign that, even as we hear it, impinges upon our time. It deals with the Reign of God, showing us how human life is affected when God brings in the divine Reign.[11]

One definition of the parable frequently cited appeared in C. H. Dodd's *Parables of the Kingdom*: "At its simplest the parable is a metaphor or simile drawn from nature or common life, arresting the hearer by its vividness or strangeness, and leaving the mind in sufficient doubt about its precise application to tease it into active thought."[12]

In this definition, Dodd alludes to some marks of the parable that we should note:

1. *The parable is secular, everyday, in its content.* It is familiar enough to stress the commonness of the elements that Jesus introduced in the parables. He spoke freely of sheep and seed, corrupted judges, and a rebellious son, of children playing in a marketplace and a poor servant being forgiven a debt he owned his employer. What perhaps gives this obvious fact more impact, however, is to recognize that only four of the forty-six parables identified in this study deal with a subject or character that is religious at all.[13] Jesus did not presuppose that the hearer was

a believer already.[14] He selected a portion of life, described an incident within life that inspired belief, and invited the hearer who had entered the situation to reflect upon it and decide upon the course his or her life was to take.

2. *The parable is a simile or metaphor.* In a parable, a comparison is made. Something that is not well known — or at least readily recognized — is compared to something that is better known. The word, "parable," is taken from a Greek verb that means simply "to throw beside" (even referring to throwing fodder beside horses!) or "to compare."

In a simile one thing is said to be *like* another: for example, "my love is like a red, red rose." A metaphor, on the other hand, says that one thing *is* another: "You are my sunshine, my only sunshine." In a simile or metaphor, two terms that are not quite comparable, are "thrown beside" one another, causing the mind and imagination to struggle with the reality that is being disclosed. This produces insight and understanding that cannot be reduced to our conventional analytical manner of speaking.[15]

When the dissimilar are "thrown" side-by-side, the conventions of language itself are temporarily put aside (what would it mean literally to say, "You are my sunshine"?) in order to jar the imagination into a fuller grasp of a reality. This is, in part, what Dodd refers to as the "strangeness" that teases us into active thought. Through that fracture of language, the light shines. A parable operates upon our imagination by means of simile and metaphor.

3. *The parable uses vivid language.* Though told with an economy of words, the parables of Jesus use vivid images that fix themselves in our memory and imagination. In the Parable of the Pharisee and the Publican, we are told just enough about the bearing and posture of the publican, standing far off, eyes downcast, beating his breast, to gain a vivid image of this penitent man and to contrast him to the Pharisee who recounted his virtue in exceeding the requirements of the Law (Luke 18:9–14).

Events that are recounted are told with such credibility that they may well have been based on actual happenings, events that had been the topic of village conversation, such as a burglary, a manager who got himself out of a jam, or a rogue who planted weeds in someone else's wheat field.[16]

4. *The parable involves the hearer as a participant.* In some

of the parables, Jesus put a question directly to the hearer and asked for a response. One example is the lawyer who asked for a scholarly opinion on the definition of the neighbor and who found himself confronted not with an answer but with a question: "Which of these three, do you think, proved neighbor to the man who fell among the robbers?" (Luke 10:36). He who thought to put the teacher to the test was himself being examined! The Parable of the Lost Sheep (Matt. 18:12–14/Luke 15:4–7) begins with the question: "What do you think?" In other words, "Put this up against your own experience of life. How does a person normally respond?" Or again, Jesus asks the hearer to judge concerning the appropriateness of the responses of two sons. "Which of the two did the will of the father?" (Matt. 21:31).

Even in instances when the question is not explicit, the parable requires participation. By its nature, it requires that we struggle with the image or story to determine in which way it depicts the Reign of God that Jesus is inaugurating.[17] The struggle and participation is not so much a struggle of the intellect as it is of the imagination. How does one feel the impact of the Parable of the Prodigal Son (Luke 15:11–32) without "standing" in the situation — feeling the situation through the life of an adventurous son, an overjoyed father, a dutiful son, and a son rejoined to his father? The point is to appropriate the joy felt by a father whose son was dead and now lived, who was lost and now was found. Similarly, the struggle in the Parable of the Unjust Judge is to appreciate the fight that the widow had on her hands in insisting upon her rights and the marvel that she won them even from a corrupt judge (Luke 18:1–8) and then to recognize how much more we can count on God to uphold those who pray constantly for divine vindication.

In contrast to other forms of teachings, the parables are situations in which we are invited to participate. To shield ourselves from the relationships and the forces of the relationship itself is to miss the point. To this extent parables are like good jokes. One function of a good joke is to present life's discontinuities, its dislocations and indignities, in such a manner that the tension caused by them is relieved. To "get" the joke is to enter into the situation and experience the relief of laughter. Nothing quite substitutes (including this explanation!) for being enough a part of the situation so that laughter comes almost involuntarily as a spontaneous response. The joke tells us what we need to know in order to appreciate the humor of the situation. If the story is a "put-down" of a self-important person, we are told that the person shortly to meet his or her downfall is an officious and conceited person. This then helps us to enter into the humor when the person receives the jolt that he or she so richly deserves. Anyone who has been surrounded by uproarious laughter and not "gotten" the joke or anyone who has tried to explain a joke to a person without a sense of humor knows the difference between entering the situation and experiencing it from inside and standing outside the situation altogether. The parable, like the joke, is a literary form that requires participation. To those who choose to stand outside its world, it has little meaning.

5. *The parable calls for a decision.* We have said that the context for the parables in Jesus' preaching was the breaking in of God's Reign. "The new age has begun and God has entered history in a new way."[18] The urgency of his mission rested in the presence of the final hour before the Reign of God became manifest. "The denouement of the world-story is come; the characters and their little histories are now in Act V; in fact, we hear twelve o'clock beginning to strike."[19] The parables were given, therefore, not for the illumination of the intellect. They were intended to summon people to a decision to live in the power of the Reign of God, to respond to God's gracious invitation of forgiveness, to put aside goods for the prize worth having above all.

The implicit call of the Parable of the Pearl or the Hidden Treasure (Matt. 13:44, 45) is to surrender every other good — including family and reputation — for the sake of the all-surpassing joy of God's Reign. The Parable of the Prodigal Son (Luke 15:11–32) called for a decision from the Pharisee who protested the entrance of the unworthy into the Reign of God. It asked him to respond to the extraordinary situation with joy and celebration rather than with grudging, petulant hostility.

JESUS' USES OF THE PARABLES

Because of the characteristics that mark the parables, they were admirably suited for use in Jesus' ministry. Within the context of Jesus' teaching, they were the most easily grasped, the most readily understood means available for making his point. They had to be so clear, so compelling that even Jesus' adversaries would have to admit the force of his argument. They were not spoken in quiet moments of withdrawal; for the most part, they were spoken in the midst of conflict and debate. They were quick thrusts and sharp ripostes to make his point even, or especially, to those who attacked him. To understand the message Jesus sought to convey by the parables, therefore, we must look at the uses to which he put them.

1. *The parables as answers to his critics, the Pharisees.* The most prominent use of the parables was in his debates with the Pharisees. Jesus' conflicts with the Pharisees were so significant in shaping the parables that we need to examine the points at issue between him and them.

The New Testament records at several points the sharp words that Jesus spoke against the Pharisees (see especially Matt. 23), but we should not assume from this that the Pharisees were always antagonistic to him. The Pharisees were more closely allied with Jesus than were other principal parties in Judaism at that time. In the Gospels, Jesus was frequently pictured as being on friendly terms with the Pharisees.[20] He attended a feast in a Pharisee's house, for example (Luke 7:36ff.). It was "some Pharisees" who came to him to warn him of Herod's plan to kill him (Luke 13:31), and it was a ruler who belonged to the Pharisees who entertained Jesus at a Sabbath meal (Luke 14:1). At least some of the Pharisees addressed Jesus with a title of respect, calling him "Teacher" (see John 11:28). In view of Jesus' denunciations of the Pharisees, it is remarkable that the Gospel writers recorded this evidence of friendship between Jesus and them.

Nor did the frequent debates that Jesus had with the Pharisees necessarily imply that they always disagreed. The Pharisees sided with Jesus against the Sadducees on the question of the resurrection (Matt. 22:23–40), and some of their number defended him publicly (John 9:16). There is evidence that the Pharisees were present when Jesus taught (Luke 5:17) and that they put searching questions to him (Luke 17:20).

Who, then, were the Pharisees? As a party in Judaism, they were likely already in existence at the time of the Maccabean

wars (c. 162 B.C.).[21] The Pharisees developed in opposition to
the Sadducees and had as their purpose the development of a
holy community, the "true Israel."[22] While the Sadducees represented a priestly party associated with the Temple, the Pharisees
were primarily a lay movement.[23] The Pharisees were instru-
mental in the development of the synagogue with its emphasis
upon prayer and the reading of Scripture and upon one's individual relationship with God. It was not by happenstance that
the apostle Paul, himself of Pharisaic background (Acts 23:6;
Phil. 3:5), preached the risen Christ at the place where the followers of the Pharisees gathered, the synagogue.[24] This was a
place likely to win a favorable hearing for the Christian Gospel.

The Pharisees won the loyalties of the common people. While
the Sadducees represented primarily the conservative nobility,
the Pharisees de-emphasized differences between people because
of class. They themselves were composed not of the aristocracy
but principally of merchants, artisans, and peasants who had no
scribal education.[25]

The Pharisees sought to extend the rule of the Torah to the
life of the whole community and placed their emphasis upon
the acquisition of merit by exceeding the requirements of the
Law. But their concerns were far broader than purity legally de-
fined. The Pharisaic communities, of which there were several in
Jerusalem, were disciplined orders directed not merely to personal rectitude in matters of the Law but to works of public
charity.[26] The Pharisees welcomed converts to Judaism[27] and
even aggressively sought them out (Matt. 23:13–15).

What, then, was the source of the conflict between the Pharisees and Jesus? Their dispute was not centrally in their interpretation of the Law. Jesus himself said that the scribes and
Pharisees "sit on Moses' seat" (Matt. 23:2), i.e., they are stew-
ards of the Law. Their dispute rested in their appraisal of what
was happening in history. At the time the Pharisees were accen-
tuating the sharp line between a purified community that is to
be the "true Israel" and the rest of the people, Jesus was pro-
claiming that God's Reign was arriving and that the ingathering
of God's great banquet for Jews and Gentiles was taking place.
For Jesus, the great outpouring of God's grace and forgiveness
was happening in the extension of table-fellowship to sinners
and the righteous alike. The gathering of the righteous and the

sinners together at one table was itself a glimpse of God's Reign. But the Pharisees held it offensive to receive sinners unless they first repented and obeyed the Law. For Jesus, the emphasis was not upon an act of repentance that would qualify one for God's Reign but upon the free, unreserved offer of forgiveness that marked its coming. Repentance was a response to grace, not its precondition![28]

Jesus taught that the extension of God's forgiveness radically altered the way in which people were to regard others. Those dismissed as "sinners" by conventional reckoning were ones who loved God much because they had been forgiven much (see the Parable of the Two Debtors, Luke 7:41–43). The opponents of Jesus were likened to the son who promised to work in his father's vineyard and did not. The sinners, by contrast, were compared to the son who at first refused to work but afterwards had a change of heart and did the work (Matt. 21:28–32).

The aim of the parables as answers to Jesus' opponents, then, was to provide glimpses of the characteristic ways in which God's Reign could be recognized when it burst upon them. They portrayed ordinary happenings to suggest a context in which one course of action is logical and necessary. The context of the coming Reign of God makes what would otherwise be extraordinary or scandalous not only permissible but necessary. The lost are found; the dead now live. It is a time for rejoicing!

2. *The parables as disclosures of God's Reign.* The effectiveness of Jesus' use of the parables in debate depended upon their capacity to depict an alternative view of the world. Jesus' aim was not to sketch the Reign of God as a means of diverting attention from this world to another. Rather, he sought to show how this very world was transmuted and illumined by the activity of God. Because God's Reign was yet to come in its fullness, Jesus showed that it could be grasped now by momentary glimpses, by fleeting intimations. He said, for example, that if we could participate in the joy of a widow who had lost a coin and then found it or could celebrate the surprise of a worker who was hired later in the day and yet received a full days' wages, then perhaps we could experience what God's Reign is like when it is encountered among us.

The Reign of God that the parables disclose is never seen directly. It is grasped — if at all — by the impact it makes upon the present world that is all around us. Perhaps it can be compared to the place of the sun in a landscape painting. The sun may never be pictured in the painting, but its impact is everywhere. Its position in the sky shapes the slant of the shadow. Its intensity and directness determine the appearance of the objects below. The colors and textures of the painting are formed by the illumination of the sun. So it is with the reality of God's Reign disclosed in the parables. While never viewed directly, it casts its light upon all the scenes that are sketched in the parables. And in the light that is shed upon them, we see a world transformed by the advent of the Reign of God.

The importance of the parables in helping us grasp the Reign of God should not be underestimated. They place us in an altered context in which new insights become possible. Discoveries and inventions in the physical sciences often come not with new facts but with a new perspective from which the facts are interpreted. Thomas Kuhn, a historian of science, has reminded us that every age of science makes its discoveries on the basis of a basic picture or model, a paradigm, for the universe. Scientists try to explain the facts that they observe within the context of that model. Scientific breakthroughs occur, however, when someone imagines a significantly different model by which to understand the world. This alternative model opens the way for new discoveries.[29]

People tried, for example, to explain the movements of the heavenly bodies using the model of a universe in which the earth was at the center. Explanations grew more and more complex in order to account for the way in which the planets moved. It was when a new model of the universe was proposed, one that pictured the sun at the center, that physicists and astronomers could account not only for the planetary movements but could understand several other phenomena that hitherto had puzzled them. Their new model opened their eyes to what they observed. Einstein himself said, "It is the theory which decides what we can observe."[30]

The parables similarly represent a new model for the world. The universe understood as orbiting around the sun is a world that is a different one from that in which the earth is the center. Likewise, the world that is now effected by the dawning of God's Reign is a new world. Regarding the world in this manner prepares us for a new grasp of who we are and what we are to do. Jesus invites us to comprehend the world in the light of the God who restores the lost, who faithfully hears those who persist in prayer, and who gives the earth as an inheritance to those who are now dispossessed. Viewed from the perspective of this model, the world disclosed by the parables is dramatically new.

3. *The parables as interpreters of Jesus' hearers.* We will notice at several points in our study of the parables that the parables interpret those who hear them. Even as we set about to discover their meaning, they open us up to scrutiny. Nothing reveals more about us as individuals than what we consider funny. Certain happenings or anecdotes set off reactions within us that move us, almost involuntarily, to laughter. Our response discloses abundant insights into the kind of persons we are, the sensitivities we possess, and the tensions we experience.

Similarly, our response to the parables reveals something about our basic stance before life. If the grace of God in bringing God's Reign has radically turned around our estimate of people, how do we respond? Do we rejoice with the dispossessed who now are exalted, or do we grudgingly protest the impropriety of it all?

To hear the parables aright is to participate in a new world. To believe is to be able to act upon the basis of that new world. Some teachings provide information so that one can participate in a new reality. The parables, on the contrary, help us to experience a new reality so that we can later explore its meanings.[31] One does not explain the heights and depths of marriage to a couple so that the fullness of its meaning is transparent as they enter matrimony. Rather, two persons commit themselves to one another unreservedly and, in the process of reflecting upon this commitment, discover one another and the meaning of their relationship. The parables likewise invite us into a world illuminated by God's action. As we place our reliance upon the world, we discover the mystery of God's Reign.

QUESTIONS AND SUGGESTED METHODS

1. What characteristics of a Pharisee would make that person considered a good church member today? What qualities would

make him or her an inadequate church member? What are the qualities we share most closely with the Pharisees?

2. T-shirts and bumper stickers are two of the most widely used media for sharing concerns or interests with others. Devise brief slogans based upon a parable that would be suitable for either or both media. Can you phrase it so that it is readily understood by someone who is not familiar with the parables? Can it lead to an opportunity to tell the story to another person? Individuals or groups may want to produce T-shirts or bumper stickers and use them as a means of sharing the parables.

3. Assign teams to read through the forty-six parables listed here, with separate assignments to each.

- *Team A* should make a list of the characters in the parables, noting, where available, the social and economic standing of each one. How many characters usually appear in a parable? What groups, if any, are over-represented or under-represented, in your view?

- *Team B* should list the general situations described in the parables. What was happening in each (finding the lost, dealing with a crisis, experiencing a sharp reversal, etc.)? What categories can be used to summarize the action of the parables?

- *Team C* should list the descriptive words that might be used in characterizing God's Reign on the basis of the parables (joy, surprise, grace, etc.). What synonyms do you find for God's Reign in the parables?

- *Team D* should record the questions that are asked of Jesus and the questions that Jesus asked. What do they reveal about Jesus and his questioners?

In the class session, the four teams might report their findings, in each instance suggesting what new insights they derived concerning Jesus' teaching from their investigation.

4. The message of Jesus in many of the parables is that the dawning of God's Reign justifies setting aside some religious conventions and rules — worthy as they are — because of the surpassing joy of God's coming Reign. What types of happenings in our culture lead people to set aside normal forms of behavior? What situations permit or require unusual acts of celebration and merriment or self-sacrifice and restraint? Note the manner in which the situation alters our notion of what is appropriate? What parallels are there from these examples to those cited by Jesus that permitted or required unusual actions?

5. Each individual and group has stories that help them to emphasize who they are as individuals or as groups. Think of the stories that help establish your identity as an individual, a family, a member of an ethnic or language group, a church, a small town person, a rural person, a city person. Are there jokes that your group tells about another group to distinguish them from you? Those who are willing may share examples of these with other individuals or with the group as a whole. How does a story establish and secure identity? How are these comparable to the parables? How different?

6. The parables are meant to be told. They are intended to be told primarily to those who are on the outside. As the study of the parables progresses, some persons may select one of the parables that speaks to them most directly and seek occasions in which that story may be shared with others. The telling of the parable may be followed by such questions as: Who are the characters? What did they do? What issues are at stake for them? With whom do you identify most in the parable? What aspects of the other characters do you find in yourself? How did Jesus' first hearers likely react?

7. The parables have been one of the richest sources of themes in the history of the graphic arts. Select a pictorial history of art (or slides or prints if you can secure them from a museum or other source) and study the manner in which the parables have been depicted by various artists. What in their depiction conveys their understandings of Jesus' message? What new insights do you receive from the painting or sculpture?

Notes

1. *Jesus' Parables and the War of Myths*, ed. James Breech (Philadelphia: Fortress, 1982), p. 76.
2. Archibald M. Hunter, *Interpreting the Parables* (Philadelphia: Westminster, 1960), p. 7.
3. Joseph Klausner, *Jesus of Nazareth: His Life, Times and Teaching*, trans. Herbert Dandy (New York: Macmillan, 1950 [1925]), p. 264.
4. There are evident differences of emphasis concerning the use of parables by rabbis who were Jesus' contemporaries. Joachim Jeremias acknowledges that they used parables but holds that Jesus' use of this medium was so unique that his parables represent something "entirely new" (*The Parables of Jesus*, trans. S. H. Hooke, 2d rev. ed. [New York: Charles Scribner's Sons, 1972], p. 12). W. O. E. Oesterley provides a history of the use of parables in the Hebrew Bible and interprets the extensive use of parables by rabbis in the time of Jesus (*The Gospel Parables in the Light of Their Jewish Background* [London: Society for Promoting Christian Knowledge, 1936], pp. 4–12). Oesterley illustrates Jesus' use of familiar themes from rabbinic parables, noting the considerably different emphasis for which they were used in Jesus' teaching. Hunter's *Interpreting the Parables* includes one section in which examples of parables used by rabbis at the time of Jesus are quoted (pp. 113–116). For other illustrations, see Eta Linnemann, *Jesus of the Parables*, trans. John Sturdy (New York: Harper & Row, 1964), pp. 18–23. John Dominic Crossan believes that the rabbinic parables that are similar to Jesus' parables were created by the rabbis after Jesus' teaching ministry (*Cliffs of Fall: Paradox and Polyvalence in the Parables of Jesus* [New York: The Seabury Press, 1980], p. 17.)
   To the present author, the evidence points strongly to the conclusion that Jesus, in employing parables, was drawing upon a general form of teaching familiar to his audience, but that in his use of parables he developed the parable into a distinctively new form. (Cf. this general conclusion in Amos Wilder, *Early Christian Rhetoric* [Cambridge: Harvard University Press, 1971], p. 90, and Warren Kissinger, *The Parables of Jesus: A History of Interpretation and Bibliography* [Metuchen, N.J.: Scarecrow Press, 1979], p. 157.) Crossan (*Cliffs of Fall*, pp. 16, 17) notes that whereas the rabbis of Jesus' day taught within the authority of a group, in the synagogue, and with canonical texts, Jesus taught without such group authority, outside the synagogue, and without canonical texts.
5. These examples suggested by T. W. Manson, *The Teaching of Jesus* (Cambridge: University Press, 1955), p. 63.

6. John Drury in his *The Parables in the Gospels* provides an extensive discussion of the general category of parables in the Hebrew Bible, including sayings, metaphors, enigmatic allegorical parables, songs of decision, a byword, and prophetic oracle (London: SPCK, 1985, pp. 7–20)

7. Linnemann, *Jesus of the Parables*, p. 20.

8. Gunther Bornkamm, *Jesus of Nazareth*, trans. Irene and Fraser McLuskey with James M. Robinson (New York: Harper & Row, 1960), p. 69.

9. Amos Wilder, *Jesus' Parables and the War of Myths* (Philadelphia: Fortress Press, 1982), p. 83.

10. John J. Vincent, *Secular Christ* (New York: Abingdon, 1968), p. 115.

11. Norman Perrin, *Rediscovering the Teaching of Jesus* (New York: Harper & Row, 1976), pp. 82–83.

12. C. H. Dodd, *Parables of the Kingdom* (London: Nisbet & Co., 1935), p. 16.

13. These four exceptions are noted by Lucetta Mowry, "Parable," *The Interpreter's Dictionary of the Bible*, ed. George A. Buttrick (New York: Abingdon, 1962).

14. Robert W. Funk, *Language, Hermeneutic, and Word of God* (New York: Harper & Row, 1966), p. 178.

15. Ibid., p. 136.

16. John R. Donahue, *The Gospel in Parable* (Philadelphia: Fortress Press, 1988), p. 10.

17. Amos Wilder, *Jesus and the War of Myths*, p. 71.

18. See Jeremias, *The Parables of Jesus*, pp. 182, 224.

19. Sallie McFague TeSelle, *Speaking in Parables* (Philadelphia: Fortress, 1975), p. 67.

20. The following summary draws upon Oesterley, *The Gospel Parables*, pp. 42ff.

21. See the history of the Pharisaic movement in Jeremias, *Jerusalem in the Time of Jesus*, trans. F. H. and C. H. Cave (Philadelphia: Fortress, 1969), pp. 246–267.

22. Ibid., p. 266.

23. Ibid., p. 256. For the contrasting viewpoint that the scribes and Pharisees are one, see Ellis Rivkin, "Pharisees," in *The Interpreter's Dictionary of the Bible*, Supplementary volume, ed. Keith Crim (Nashville: Abingdon, 1976), p. 659.

24. Rivkin, "Pharisees," p. 661.

25. Jeremias, *Jerusalem in the Time of Jesus*, p. 259.

26. Ibid., p. 250.

27. Rivkin, "Pharisees," p. 660.

28. Frederick H. Borsch, speaking of the Parable of the Lost Sheep (Matt. 18:12–14/Luke 15:4–7) comments: "The challenge of the parable...is not just to Judaism but to every form of religion which requires repentance or some other way of preparing for God's acceptance before that acceptance can come" (*Many Things in Parables* [Philadelphia: Fortress Press, 1988], pp. 60–61).

29. Cf. Thomas Kuhn, *The Structure of Scientific Revolutions* (Chicago: University of Chicago Press, 1962). See also Ian G. Barbour, *Myths, Models and Paradigms* (New York: Harper & Row, 1974).

30. Quoted in Daniel Bell, *The Coming of the Post-Industrial Society* (New York: Basic Books, 1973), p. 9.

31. John Dominic Crossan, *In Parables: The Challenge of the Historical Jesus* (New York: Harper & Row, 1973), p. 14.

Part II

Entering God's Reign

Chapter 3

The Irruption of God's Reign

To irrupt is to "rush in forcibly or violently."[1] Perhaps this is the most adequate manner in which to describe the nature of the Reign of God as it is glimpsed in the parables of Jesus. The Reign of God will come suddenly from without. When it comes, it will be utterly different from the former age. Its coming will constitute God's final and decisive assault upon the forces of Satan and will institute that age in which God's sovereignty will be visible for all.

The Gospel writers tell us that, with Jesus' appearance, the decisive struggle between God and the satanic forces began. The satanic powers were exhibited by demons, disease, demon possession, insanity, and other aberrations.[2] The demons immediately recognized that Jesus was the one appointed by God because they, like him, were from the supernatural realm. Jesus went about healing, casting out evil spirits, and even walked over the water during a storm. While terrible suffering lay ahead, the forces of Satan were overcome in him; Satan was said to have fallen from the sky (Luke 10:18).

Some convictions seemed to be clear to the writers of the Gospels about this irrupting Reign of God. First, *it would come with terrible suffering*. The struggle of God against Satan would visit immense suffering upon humans and nature; the forces of evil would resist the imposition of God's rightful rule on the world. The petitions in the Lord's Prayer, "Lead us not into temptation, but deliver us from evil," refer to the eschatological trial and the suffering entailed in it (Matt. 10:23). Second,

Jesus sought to gather up a *community* prepared to receive God's Reign and to live in its light. Third, the *punishment* was severe for those who were oblivious to the nature of the time and thus were caught unprepared when it came swiftly upon them.

To the consternation of his own disciples, Jesus said that he would not escape his portion of the suffering. He linked his coming suffering with their recognition that he was the Christ (Mark 8:29–31/Matt. 16:16/Luke 9:20; see also Isaiah 42:1).[3] After his death, the final consummation would come; it would come within the lifetime of those who heard him. The old age would end and the new one begin. The Son of Man would be vindicated by God and would return with angels to exercise his glory (Matt. 19:28; 24:39; 25:31; Luke 17:30; 18:8).[4]

Against this background, we consider three clusters of parables of Jesus that treat the theme of the irrupting Reign of God. Three factors related to the irruption of God's Reign serve as focus for this chapter: the assault on Satan's power, the suddenness of its coming, and the incompatibility with the old age.

THE ASSAULT ON SATANIC POWERS

Parables of the House and Kingdom Divided
and the Strong Man's House
(Matt. 12:25–29 / Mark 3:23–27 / Luke 11:17–23)

The irruption of the Reign of God implied that God, through the "anointed one," the Christ, was now entering the last and decisive struggle with the forces of disease, oppression, and alienation. In Jesus' day, those forces were not regarded as unconnected realities with which to deal. They were thought to represent the demonic, which was organized into a network of demons. It was ruled by the prince of demons and carried on a coordinated campaign to accomplish satanic purposes.

We should be very cautious about discarding these categories — admittedly a part of a worldview different from our own — as hopelessly outdated notions. While we are not likely to speak of demons and their prince, we know that the evils of disease, war, oppression, and injustice are not isolated or the products of individual ill will. They are rather, as we say, "systemic" in their nature. War and hunger are interconnected. It is impossible to confront the racism or sexism that distorts the oppressor and the oppressed without reckoning with the organized greed that capitalizes on such oppression. If we address the question of energy, we must consider, at the same time, the implications for our use of diminishing resources upon those dependent upon those same resources for food and survival. The forces that exacerbate suffering are not individual; they are interconnected. Our struggle with them must be addressed to the forces of evil as a system and not as isolated aberrations or "mistakes."

The biblical insight into the interconnectedness and willfulness of evil is symbolized in the image of a variety of demonic forces forged into an alliance under their prince. Matthew and Luke both report that the Parable of the House and Kingdom Divided was spoken immediately after Jesus healed a man who was unable to talk. (Matthew adds that the man was also blind.) The evangelists both assumed that the cause of the affliction was the habitation of a demonic spirit. They report that Jesus cast out the evil spirit, the man talked (and saw), and the crowds were amazed (Matt. 12:22–23/Luke 11:14).

For Matthew the healing formed the third in a series of acts of Jesus that occasioned a protest from the Pharisees. Earlier, Jesus had plucked grain (Matt. 12:1–2) and healed a man with a withered hand on the Sabbath (12:9–14).

When Jesus cast out the evil spirit, the Pharisees charged that he accomplished this wonder by the power of the prince of the demonic world, Beelzebul (Matt. 12:24/Mark 3:22/Luke 11:15). The name, a corruption for the name of the god of Ekron (2 Kings 1:2), meant "lord of the house." It conveyed the image of Satan as the unrightful holder of a territory until his power was broken by one stronger than he.[5]

We should note here that not even Jesus' opponents were denying his ability to work wonders. Neither did Jesus claim that only he worked wonders. He later said that some of their number ("your sons") also cast out demons (Matt. 12:27/Luke 11:19).

Those who believe that Jesus was God's anointed one principally because of his wonder-working powers should recognize that the evangelists did not believe that these powers in themselves set him apart from others. At issue was not his capacity to cast out demons but the authority by which this was done. It was not that the wonders themselves made Jesus significant; rather, it was who he was, his position in God's acts in history, which gave earth-shaking significance to his actions. His casting out of demons was the sign of the opening of the decisive struggle in which all the interconnected forces of evil would be overcome.

The attack of Jesus' opponents was that he was practicing some sort of magic by powers given to him by the prince of the satanic powers. He was accused of being in alliance with Satan. Jesus' response, characteristically, was a brief parable or metaphor. Any kingdom or city or house with a civil war going on within it cannot stand. It will destroy itself. In effect, Jesus said, "If Satan is giving me the power to cast out satanic forces from people such as this man who is blind and dumb, then how can Satan's kingdom stand? He is fighting against himself and will bring on his own ruin. Anyone knows that Satan is too crafty to bring about the destruction of his own kingdom of evil. "No," Jesus continued, "my casting out demons is not the sign of an alliance with Satan. My casting out of demons by the Spirit of God is a sign that the Reign of God has come in your midst" (see Matt. 18:28/Luke 11:20).

The image of the prince of demons as "lord of the house" ties in closely with the parable that follows immediately in all three Gospels. Obviously, one does not enter a strong man's house and carry off his possessions until one first overcomes him and binds him up. The implication of the parable was that Satan's force had been overcome already. Jesus' casting out demons was his seizing what had been Satan's and liberating it. This liberation was an element of the coming of God's Reign.

Far from being a minion of Satan, Jesus was arrayed against him on behalf of God's Reign. Furthermore, Satan's power had now been conquered. As God's Reign dawned, his illegitimate holdings would now be seized.

THE SUDDENNESS OF THE COMING OF GOD'S REIGN

While the theme of the lightning-quick coming of the Reign of God is present in several of the parables, the five parables in this section have this as their primary emphasis. We can read these parables at two levels. First, we can discern in them the original warning of Jesus about the impending eschatological hour, when the Reign of God would come bringing joy for those prepared and punishment for those who were not. Here the exhortation is to be alert and to exercise foresight and prudence so that the cataclysmic hour will not find one unready for it. The coming of God's Reign is compared to a late-night arrival at the door, a master returning from a party, a bridegroom, and a thief.

Second, these parables reveal the struggle of the early church to understand the significance of these parables for their situation. Christians lived in the steady expectation of the return of the Lord. More than a generation had passed since the crucifixion and resurrection, but Jesus had not returned in kingly glory in the manner they had expected. Some began to question and to grow impatient.

Expectations for God's direct intervention and the return of Jesus were stirred once again by the desperation experienced as Rome defeated a Jewish uprising in A.D. 66–70. The human suffering imposed by the Roman siege of the city of Jerusalem was accompanied by the desecration of the Temple by Roman forces. Surely this, thought many, was the "desolating sacrilege" that Jesus said would precede the Son of Man's return (Mark 13:14, 26). But the Lord did not return. The event that many had thought would take place within the lifetime of those who has heard Jesus had not happened, and many of the eyewitnesses had died.

It was in this situation that the early church interpreted the meaning of the parables. As the church remembered and interpreted the words of Jesus, some of the emphasis of the parables likely shifted.[6] Parables that first spoke of an imminent in-rushing event for which they had to be prepared now were interpreted in more long-range perspective. Allusions were made to a delay in the Lord's return and to the consequent need for patience. Readers were urged neither to despair of the Lord's return nor to be found unprepared when he appeared. In this section, we consider some of the parables that address the matter of the suddenness of the coming of God's Reign. We shall notice, as well, the manner in which these parables were applied to the life of the early church.

The Parable of the Doorkeeper
(Mark 13:33–37 / Luke 12:35–38;
cf. also Luke 19:12–13 and Matt. 25:14–15b)

The theme of the doorkeeper and the servants charged with responsibility appears at several points in the Gospels. In Matthew 25:14–15b, very little of the parable remains. It appears in fullest fashion in Luke 12:35–38. The theme is repeated in Luke 19:12–13. Behind the various versions, one plot is found. A man — wealthy enough to afford servants — leaves his house to attend a party, perhaps a wedding party.[7] He charges the one who was doorkeeper to keep watch so that when the master of the house returns he will have help.

Presumably, the later the master's return from the party, the more likely he will need help. Yet, the later the hour, the more difficult it will be for the doorkeeper to stay awake and alert. The one who is faithful will be rewarded by his master, according to Luke (12:37), by being given a meal (a reference to the Messianic Banquet).

The force of the parable depends upon the comparison between the unexpectedness of the master's return and the consequent need to be constantly alert, and the plight of the person who awaits God's irrupting Reign. Jesus likely applied this to the scribes, emphasizing the charge that they have been given and the imminent, abrupt event that was going to judge them and find them wanting in their stewardship.[8]

The same basic story is interpreted in a variety of ways in the Gospels. In Mark, the master of the household is not just away for the evening; he has left on a journey (Mark 13:34). A much longer absence is obviously involved. He divided up the responsibilities among his household staff, commanding the doorkeeper to keep watch (Mark 13:34). And, once again, the servant is enjoined to stay awake so that when the master returned at any part of the night, someone would be prepared to receive him.[9]

The length of time before the return of the master of the household is highly uncertain in some versions of the parable. Whereas Luke suggests that he will return at some time during the evening — whether sooner or later — Matthew and Mark indicate that neither the day nor the hour is known. For them it is not simply a matter of staying alert for one evening. What is required instead is a life of constant vigilance so that, whether the master comes soon or far off in the future, the faithful will be ready. And Luke adds that when he returns he will sit at table with the servant, reminding the believers of the great banquet that awaits them when the Lord returns (Luke 12:37).[10]

We have said that the various versions of this parable of Jesus reflect the need for the early church to interpret Jesus' message in relation to their own situation. Originally, Jesus spoke of the sudden coming of God's Reign, the great crisis that would precede its fulfillment. He urged people to be ready when it appeared. But when it did not appear, the church had to adjust to a more long-range perspective. Clearly the doorkeeper cannot stand beside the door for an indefinite period. He must be about his normal chores *while* he anticipates the master's need. Their entire focus could not be on watching for the coming of the Lord. The pressing needs of the church required them to assume their ongoing responsibilities. Sometimes such drastic events as the fall of Jerusalem in A.D. 70 inspired a flurry of speculations about the impending arrival of the Lord,[11] but they interpreted these parables to exhort them to patience while waiting for the Lord. They were not to be consumed with constant excitement about the Lord's return; neither were they to flag in their faithfulness to the duties that had been assigned to them.

The image that emerges from this parable is that of the servant who is alert and ready for action. His loins are girded (Luke 12:35); the long robes are tucked in girdles so that he is ready to move swiftly. His lamps are burning so that he will not be detained by the laborious process of lighting a torch (without matches). All things are ready for quick action in the face of the prospect of the master's imminent return.

The Parable of the Faithful and Wise Servant
(Matt. 24:45–51 / Luke 12:42–46)

In Luke's Gospel, the Parable of the Doorkeeper leads directly to the Parable of the Faithful and Wise Servant. The parable begins typically with a question — in this case a question in response to Peter's question (Luke 12:41): "Who then is the faithful and wise steward, whom his master will set over his household, to give them their portion of food at the proper time?" (Luke 12:42/Matt. 24:45).

In this case, the "faithful and wise steward" is in a considerably more responsible position than the word "servant" (*doulos* or slave) in Matthew would imply. The power and authority of the master are invested in him while the master is away. The manager acts in the place of the master during his absence and thus fills a highly responsible position. His is the responsibility of distributing weekly or monthly rations of food to all on the estate. Luke terms him an *oikonomos* or "manager of the estate" a title more fitting for the responsibilities described. For good or ill, he is given virtually total power over the rest of the staff.[12]

The reward promised the faithful manager is yet wider responsibilities (Matt. 24:47/Luke 12:44), but the penalties for unfaithfulness are severe. Should the manager think that the delay in his master's return provides him an unchecked opportunity to feast and become drunk (perhaps on the rations intended for the servants!), he will be faced with sudden and drastic punishment when the master finally returns. Such deliberate unfaithfulness to solemn responsibility moves the master when he returns abruptly, surprising his drunken manager, to "cut him in two." (This expression, usually interpreted as a metaphor for a severe beating, may have been meant literally.)[13]

The force of this parable centers upon a sudden cataclysmic visit in which one is either vindicated or found severely wanting. In the context of Jesus' teaching, this parable may have been aimed first at the scribes who were charged with weighty responsibilities under the Law but who failed to recognize the appearance of God's Reign when it came.[14] But as the early church developed and struggled with the meaning of Jesus' words for its own situation, the parables often were applied to the church itself, particularly to those who were in positions of leadership. The parable came to be interpreted as a warning to the church leaders to be diligent in exercising their responsibility. Lest they should use the delay in the Lord's return as an opportunity to betray their trust, they were warned of the punishment visited upon the partying manager who indulged himself and mistreated those within his authority.

The Parable of the Burglar
(Matt. 24:42–44 / Luke 12:39–40)

Jesus used yet other metaphors to describe the necessity of being alert to the times and not allowing the impending crisis to overtake his hearers unaware. Both Matthew and Luke include the image of a burglar working in the dark by stealth. The focus of the parable is not the malevolence of the thief but the suddenness of his coming and the consequent need for preparedness. Jesus used his image to warn of the swift and unexpected nature of the coming of the Reign of God.[15]

Both Matthew and Luke use a figure concerning the days of Noah that helps us to understand the Parable of the Burglar. Matthew indicated that he believed that the two were closely related by placing the figure in conjunction with the parable. In this figure, Jesus spoke of those who lived in the days of Noah and how they went about their customary business. "They ate, they drank, they married, they were given in marriage, until the day when Noah entered the ark, and the flood came and destroyed them all" (Luke 17:27, paralleled in Matt. 24:38–39). Similarly, in the days of Lot, people were buying and selling, planting and building when the destruction of fire and brimstone descended upon them and they were destroyed (Luke 17:28–29).

These figures, uttered in the context of Jesus' ministry, were obviously intended to warn those who complacently went about their daily business of the sudden and swift destruction that would descend upon them. Preoccupied as they were with the details of their lives, they were completely mindless of the judgment of the Reign of God already drawing near. But it would soon irrupt with punishment and distress for those who were not prepared. To them the word was to be watchful and alert lest the flood should engulf them or a thief assault them in the night.[16]

The Parable of the Fig Tree
(Matt. 24:32f. / Mark 13:28f. / Luke 21:29–31)

While the budding of a tree is not a swift instantaneous happening, it likewise represents an important figure depicting the advent of God's Reign. The Parable of the Fig Tree is set by all of the first three evangelists in the midst of a long warning about the perils of the end time. Jesus has already predicted the destruction of the Temple (Luke 21:6) and continues to warn of the sufferings that are to befall. The appearance of such sufferings, says Jesus, is the sure sign that the Reign of God is near (Matt. 24:33/Mark 13:29/Luke 21:31).

Just as the tender growth of a tree in the spring signals the imminent bursting forth of the blossom, so those who see these sufferings about them will know that the Reign of God is near. There will be no more delay than the seeming instant between the tender shoot and the bud. All three evangelists conclude by declaring that all this will take place in the present generation (Matt. 23:34–36/Mark 13:30–32/Luke 21:32–33), though cautioning, in Matthew and Mark, that only God knows the exact day and hour at which it will occur.

The Parable of the Ten Maidens
(Matt. 25:1–13)

The Parable of the Ten Maidens, the last of the parables cited here to portray the suddenness of the coming of God's Reign, reveals wedding customs in a Palestinian village. The force of the parable as originally given doubtless stressed not only the suddenness of the bridegroom's return but the obligation for those who awaited him to exercise responsibility so that they would be prepared for the significant moment and not be locked out of the festivities that were to follow.

The time of a wedding in Jesus' day was one of communal celebration. The bride and groom presided over festivities sometimes lasting a week. Members of the wedding party were excused from such serious obligations as fasting and the study of the Law.[17] Jesus himself referred to the suspension of fasting during the time set aside for a wedding celebration (Matt. 9:15/ Mark 2:19/Luke 5:34).

The event referred to in the parable was the final step in the marriage of a couple.[18] The first step was the engagement, arranged between the fathers of the two marriage partners. Next, there was the betrothal, at which time the couple exchanged vows and the man made payments to the father of the bride and presented her with a gift. The couple was then considered legally married. Any rupture of the marriage at that time was considered on the same basis as a divorce. Death of the man during the period meant that the woman was classified as a widow. Yet the marriage was not consummated until more than a year later when the final wedding festivities took place. On the day agreed upon, wedding festivities were held in the house of the bride.[19] In the evening, the bridegroom went to the home of the bride. After many delays, the bride and the bridegroom walked in procession to the bridegroom's father's house. While they were on the way, those who had waited for just this occasion rushed out to greet them with torches, and, flooded with light, they made their way to the house to enjoy the wedding banquet and the dancing that was to follow.

Frequently the couple was delayed in its return. In modern times there is even a matter of pride in the delay, since it implies that the parents of the bride are seeking yet more costly gifts in exchange for the bride. The groom may take pride in the reluctance of the parents to part with their daughter.[20]

Central to the parable, therefore, are the factors of delay in the groom's return and the prudence exhibited by the wise so that they would take that delay into account. Perhaps the parable originally focused upon the surprise and suddenness with which the shout came at midnight, "They're on their way, they're coming!" Villagers knew of the false warnings shouted out by pranksters. As the parable was interpreted later in the church's situation, the emphasis fell more upon the extent of the delay and the need for prudence. The bride is not mentioned in the procession, as it is related by the parable, presumably to make the parable focus more upon the figure of the groom, which came to be interpreted as an allegorical reference to Christ (2 Cor. 11:2). The early church, faced with periodic announcements that the Lord's return was about to happen, could identify with the maidens who endured one false report after another that the procession was on its way. The church had adjusted itself to a lengthy wait. Even the wise maidens went to sleep!

In contrast to some of the other parables focusing upon this theme, the main emphasis is upon preparedness and prudence. When the cry is heard, it is too late to trim away the burned portion of the wicks, seek out more oil, and relight the torch to go to meet the groom. At that moment, those wise enough to have carried extra oil will be able to join the procession and take part in the great feast that is to follow (suggesting the Messianic Banquet that will accompany the institution of God's Reign). The foolish, on the other hand, can have no more share of the oil reserves, since the extra flasks of oil are probably not enough to serve them all. Hence, at the most critical time, just when they need them most, the lamps of the foolish maidens are flickering and ready to go out. They are told — even at night! — to go out to buy more oil. The net result is that they miss the procession and are excluded from the festivities that follow.

Whether the parable is interpreted by its context in Jesus' history or by the early church's expectation of the return of the Lord, the meaning is clear. The coming of the awaited moment is imminent. It may come with a cry even when people are sleeping. The crucial test will be whether or not the hearers are prepared for that moment. Those who are prepared will enter into the joy of God's Reign; those who are foolish will be disowned (Matt. 25:12) and excluded from God's Reign. The sudden irruption of God's Reign presents the faith with their most critical test.

INCOMPATIBILITY OF THE NEW AND THE OLD

*The Parables of New Patches on Old Garments
and New Wine / New Wineskins
(Matt. 9:16, 17 / Mark 2:21, 22 / Luke 5:36–39)*

The parables of the New Patches and New Wine stress the conflict between the two ages. The garment referred to is not only old; it is ragged and shredded. The patch is made of material that is new and not yet shrunk. Anyone would know that such a patch would never work! The new patch when it shrank would pull away from the ragged cloth, making a condition worse than the first. Similarly, anyone on hearing the parable spoken would know immediately that an old leather wineskin, grown cracked and brittle with age, would be a totally unsuitable container for new wine, which would expand in the process of fermentation.

All these images address the question of the incompatibility of two entities that are unlike. The force of the parable is neither to disown the Jewish heritage nor to show disdain for it. The point was that a dramatic new action of God had taken place that made a wholly different set of responses appropriate. Since God was ushering in God's Reign there was to be a decisive break with the responses appropriate to another age. No longer would it suffice alone to honor the traditional patterns of religious devotion.

The parables considered in this chapter have provided glimpses of the manner in which the Reign of God appears. Because they *are* parables rather than propositions, we cannot derive from them a series of characteristics of God's Reign that summarize the parables themselves. What we do have are a series of fragmentary pictures composed of comparisons drawn from everyday life. In living through these parables, we experience what it means to be asleep, ill prepared, or complacent and then find that, in an instant, an event of surpassing importance has come upon us. The word is to be alert to the significance of what God is bringing to pass. Matters of drastic importance are right now at our door. Those who are awake and sober will be prepared when God's Reign dawns.

QUESTIONS AND SUGGESTED METHODS

1. In this chapter and in the next several that follow, we are looking at individual parables dealing with a common theme. Individuals or groups might begin now to develop symbols or a "logo" for a parable suitable for mounting on a banner or on a poster. Individuals could take a word for the themes of chapters 3–6 and group symbols for the appropriate parables around each theme. Themes such as "warning" or "be alert" might be used for this chapter, with such themes as "joy," "reversal," "response," and "assurance" for the ones that follow.

2. Jesus depicted instances of people at ease and complacent with their normal business, unaware that a sudden and unexpected event was shortly to come upon them. What symbols would you select from current magazines or newspapers of the complacent life? What are the symbols for pressing issues that will likely invade that complacency? Symbols may be clipped from newspapers or magazines. Others may take pictures with self-developing film and form photo collages. How, if at all, is the Reign of God visible in the issues that break us out of our complacency?

3. In the New Testament, satanic powers were said to reside in individuals and torment them. They also understood that these powers were not merely individual but that they were linked together in alliances. What terms, scientific or other, do we have for describing the difficulties that people have when, as we say, "something gets into them"? How do the forces of evil actually reinforce one another? Are there expressions or theories that are used today to explain the conspiracy to evil that we see in our society?

4. The demon-possessed were thought to have recognized who Jesus was first because they, like him, were from the supernatural world. Can you think of examples now in which people who are extraordinary in some fashion are thought to recognize the truth before the rest of us? What terms do we use for people that the Bible called the demon-possessed?

5. Folk songs in some of our history have given warnings of imminent disaster if drastic steps are not taken. Can you think of any songs in our time that give such warnings? Have you seen such warnings in short stories or films? Individuals may wish to sing or play such songs on record or tape players.

6. Two persons together with a narrator could read "The Last Word,"[21] a brief drama that serves as an example of a twentieth-century warning. How does it compare and contrast with the parables of warning that Jesus told?

Notes

1. *Webster's New Collegiate Dictionary* (Springfield, Massachusetts: Merriam-Webster, 1977).

2. D. E. Nineham, *The Gospel of St. Mark* (Baltimore: Penguin Books, 1969), p. 45.

3. Howard C. Kee, *Jesus in History*, rev. ed., (New York: Harcourt Brace Jovanovich, 1977 [1970]), p. 151.

4. For example, Mark 8:38; 9:9; 13:26; Matt. 12:40/Luke 11:30; Matt. 24:27/Luke 17:24; Matt. 24:37/Luke 17:26; Matt. 24:44/Luke 12:40; Matt. 10:23; 13:41; 19:28; 24:39; 25:31; Luke 17:30; Luke 18:8. See Alan Richardson, *An Introduction to the Theology of the New Testament* (New York: Harper & Brothers, 1958), p. 134.

5. G. B. Caird, *The Gospel of St. Luke* (Baltimore: Penguin Books, 1963), p. 154.

6. Most contemporary students of the parables recognize shifts of interpretation of the parables in keeping with the situation experienced by first-century Christians. It was natural and necessary for them, or for us, to interpret the parables in the context of their own situation. Joachim Jeremias has described the way he believes the tradition of Jesus' parables changed as Christians applied them to their own situation (*Parables of Jesus*, trans. S. H. Hooke, 2d rev. ed. (New York: Charles Scribner's Sons, 1972), pp. 48ff.). The argument of Jeremias that we can develop a generally reliable conclusion about how the parable in question fit into the message and ministry is one the present author finds convincing, and it forms a basic working hypothesis for this study. For the boldest critique of this position, see John Drury, *The Parables in the Gospels* (London: SPCK, 1985). See also an approach to each of the three evangelists' treatments of the parables in Charles E. Carlston, *The Parables of the Triple Tradition* (Philadelphia: Fortress Press, 1975).

7. John Dominic Crossan, *In Parables* (New York: Harper & Row, 1973), p. 99.

8. Joachim Jeremias, *The Parables of Jesus*, p. 166.

9. In these two versions of the parable, Luke follows the Jewish method of reckoning the hours between 6:00 p.m. and 6:00 a.m. into three watches; Mark, perhaps writing for a Roman audience, divided it into four, the customary Roman division.

10. Jeremias, *The Parables of Jesus*, p. 55.

11. See Nineham, *The Gospel of St. Mark*, pp. 361–362.

12. Alfred Plummer, *A Critical and Exegetical Commentary on the Gospel According to Luke* (New York: Charles Scribner's Sons, 1900), p. 332.

13. Ibid. See also C. H. Dodd, *Parables of the Kingdom* (London: Nisbet & Co., 1935), p. 159, and Manson, *The Sayings of Jesus* (London: SCM Press, 1937, 1961), p. 118.

14. See Jeremias, *The Parables of Jesus*, p. 166; Archibald Hunter, *Interpreting the Parables* (Philadelphia: Westminster, 1960), p. 79; and Dodd, *Parables of the Kingdom*, p. 154.

15. The apostle Paul uses the same figure in his first letter to the church at Thessalonica (5:2). This shows that Paul was familiar with a tradition of Jesus' teaching as it was incorporated in early Christian preaching (later incorporated into the Gospels) that included this parable. See also Dodd, *Parables of the Kingdom*, p. 168.

16. Dodd, *Parables of the Kingdom*, p. 170.

17. Nineham, *The Gospel of St. Mark*, p. 101.

18. See the description of marriage customs in W. O. E. Oesterley, *The Gospel Parables in the Light of Their Jewish Background* (London: Society for Promoting Christian Knowledge, 1936), pp. 134ff.

19. Jeremias, *The Parables of Jesus*, p. 173.

20. Ibid., pp. 173–174.

21. James Broughton, "The Last Word: Or, What to Say about It," in *Religious Drama 3*, ed. Marvin Halverson (New York: Meridian Books, 1959), pp. 17–28.

Chapter 4

The Joy of God's Reign

While God's Reign will not come without suffering, it holds the prospect for abiding joy. Therefore, the symbols of God's Reign include that of the marriage celebration, the banquet, the harvest, healing the sick, and raising the dead. The joy of God's Reign is also represented in the parables as springing both from the recovery of the lost and from the discovery of the new.

The context of three parables about recovery of the lost, the Lost Sheep, the Lost Coin, and the Prodigal Son, is set by Luke: "Tax collectors and sinners" were gathering around Jesus and the Pharisees talked among themselves, "This man receives sinners and eats with them" (Luke 15:1–2). The language used carried the connotation that Jesus not only received but welcomed the tax collectors and sinners. One translation of it reads: "This man takes pleasure in tax-collectors and sinners and feasts with them."[1]

We are dependent as much upon what Jesus did — particularly his association with the disreputable — as upon what he said when we attempt to understand his role as the bearer of God's Reign. His actions, as well as his words, represented the coming of God's Rule. Indeed, it is only through an understanding of his actions that we can begin to comprehend why he so outraged the authorities that they turned him over to Rome to receive the death penalty.

The single action that dominated the minds of the Gospel writers, of course, was Jesus' resolute confrontation of the reli-

gious and political leaders at the center of their strength, Jerusalem, and his persistence in that mission even to the ignominy
of a public execution. Jesus' death and resurrection provide the
focus for the Gospels and dominate their telling of the Good
News.

Clearly, the actions that most infuriated those in authority were his choices of companions and associates. The people
whom Jesus helped were the outcasts of the society, the marginal
people, people who according to the prejudices and prevailing
assumptions of the time were outside the circle of acceptability.
They were

> sick people who, according to the current doctrine of retri-
> bution, must bear their disease as a punishment for some
> sin committed; demoniacs, that is to say, those possessed
> of demons; those attacked by leprosy, the "first-born of
> death," to whom life in companionship with others is de-
> nied; Gentiles, who have no share in the privileges of Israel;
> women and children who do not count for anything in the
> community; and really bad people, the guilty, whom the
> good man assiduously holds at a distance.[2]

Many of those with whom Jesus associated failed by any test to
measure up to prevailing standards of respectability. They were
uneducated and ignorant, which is to say that they had not for-
mally studied the Scriptures and were unschooled in the Law.
They were not meticulous in the rigorous demands of Temple
observance; therefore, they were unclean and sinners. They were
not the powerful who could defend themselves; many were like
the poor widow who had to take heroic measures to get justice for herself (Luke 18:1–8). Among those with whom Jesus
associated were those considered to be irreligious, immoral, un-
patriotic, unethical in business, unclean in ritual observance,
and uneducated.

What was utterly scandalous was that Jesus not only defended such action but said that this was what the Reign of
God was about. Not sentimentalizing about the "noble poor"
and never denying the reality of sin, Jesus nevertheless insisted
that God's Reign is marked by the free extension of forgiveness
to those who have offended. This forgiveness is not granted as

a response to repentance but as the very condition by which it takes place.

Jesus did not abide by the rigid proscription against men associating with women. In Palestine, it was considered disgraceful for a scholar to speak to a woman on the street. Legally a woman was regarded on a level with slaves and children and had identity only through a male figure who was her lord and master. Among Jesus' contemporaries there was joy at the birth of a son; the coming of a daughter was greeted with indifference.[3] Yet, in spite of their lowly standing, Jesus had women as followers (Mark 15:41) and accorded women equal footing with men (Matt. 21:31–32). He publicly criticized the divorce laws as coming out of the hardness of their hearts. He associated with a woman known as a sinner when he allowed her to wash his feet with her tears and wipe them with her hair (Luke 7:36–50). He identified himself with those who responded to God's Reign, saying that they were his family. Those who "hear the word of God and do it," said Jesus, are my mother and brothers (Luke 8:21).

The most outrageous actions in the view of many of Jesus' critics were not only his dubious associations but his readiness to mingle with extortioners, sinners, and the irreligious even at his meals. Eating was a form of social interaction calling for scrupulous care for the Jew. Unusual precautions were required to assure that the food served and the associations surrounding it were in keeping with the requirements of the Law. Furthermore, to be invited into a person's home for a meal was a sign of honor and acceptance. Noblemen, as an act of generosity, might invite the poor into their home to eat, but they could not corrupt themselves by sitting down at table with them.[4]

To associate with tax collectors and sinners at meals was an offense both to religious and to patriotic sensitivities. The tax collectors were minor officials of an imperialistic power. They were regarded as traitors to their own people and viewed as crooks and extortioners. As employees of a heathen government, they were in such constant contact with the heathen that it was unthinkable that they could faithfully keep the Law.[5] Generally, sinners were in two categories (see Luke 18:11): (1) People whose life was immoral, such as adulterers or swindlers, and (2) persons in one of the dishonorable occupations who were on that account deprived of their right to hold office or to testify at legal proceedings. This latter category included tax collectors, shepherds, donkey-drivers, peddlers, and others.[6]

It was just such people as these who were included among those with whom Jesus ate. He actually "partied" with sinners, for his meals with sinners were times of joy and celebration.[7] He invited himself to the home of the rich Zacchaeus, and thus honored the man who was chief of the tax collectors (Luke 19:1–10). He asked sinners and tax collectors to eat with him in his own house and mingled these guests with his own inner circle of disciples. No wonder the charge was frequently leveled against him that he repeated with his own lips: "Behold, a glutton and a drunkard, a friend of tax collectors and sinners!" (Matt. 11:19).

Jesus' participation in acts offensive to every sensitivity does not mean that he had disdain for the Law or that he was insensitive to moral distinctions. The overpowering reality that made such actions fitting and necessary was the breaking in of God's Reign and, with it, the extension of forgiveness. Now the Pharisee and the tax collector, the sinner and the righteous one could come together in joyous anticipation of God's Messianic Banquet.

Each meal that Jesus had with his friends became an anticipation of God's Reign. The gathering of diverse people together at a common table, far from being a violation of God's purposes, was, said Jesus, a sign of their fulfillment. It symbolized the joys of God's Reign; and, as at the Last Supper, it looked toward and celebrated by anticipation the Reign of God. In these meals that broke down the barriers that conventionally separated people, the force of God's Reign was making itself felt in the present.

THE RETURN OF THE LOST

The Parable of the Lost Sheep
(Matt. 18:12–14 / Luke 15:4–7)

In response to the murmurings of the Pharisees, Jesus pressed the question to the Pharisees themselves, asking their judgment on two natural situations in which joy is in order, the recovery of a lost sheep and a lost coin. They had made the charge against

Jesus. They, in turn, were asked to render a judgment about appropriate behavior for a shepherd and a woman.

It is telling, of course, that Jesus selected as models of the joy of God's Reign two persons who were themselves outcasts. Consider the instance of the shepherd. Shepherds were themselves a part of a proscribed occupation. As such they were categorized as unclean and as sinners. They were considered to be dishonest and thieving.[8] Repentance was thought to be especially hard for herdsmen because they could not know exactly all those whom they had cheated and those therefore to whom they must make amends.[9] The account of the shepherd seeking the lost sheep reflected not only his fidelity to his sheep but also the reality that he had to bring back the sheep (or its remains if it had been killed) in order to prove that he had not sold the sheep and pocketed the money. The parable reflects the low level of the shepherd's credibility![10]

By telling the parable, Jesus asked the objecting Pharisee to enter the story and consider himself a sinner: "What man of you, having a hundred sheep..." (Luke 15:4). The shock to the Pharisaic sensibility could have been lessened if Jesus had put it: "Which man of you owning a hundred sheep, if he heard that the hired shepherd had lost one, would he not summon the shepherd and demand that the sheep be found under threat of fine?"[11] But Jesus asked them, as a condition for entertaining the comparison, to put themselves in the position of the very sinner whose presence with Jesus scandalized them!

In addition to religious sensibilities that were offended, it was a serious socio-economic "come-down" to suggest that middle-class Pharisees imagine themselves in a lower-class occupation. In Palestinian culture, there was a rigid scale of status according to occupation.[12] Perhaps it is only a mild overstatement to compare Jesus' opening question to the pastor who might introduce a sermon with the question, "Which of you, being a drug dealer or prostitute, would...." As the story unfolds, the shepherd, of course, becomes the central figure in the depiction of the joy of God's Reign.

The shepherd had one hundred sheep, a moderately large flock. Ordinarily a shepherd who owned one hundred sheep would be wealthy enough to hire someone to tend them for him, or consign them to a less wealthy member of the family

sinner
also the owner

to tend.[13] Yet it is clear that the shepherd who tended the sheep in this parable was also the owner. Jesus' hearers would have assumed that the shepherd combined his own sheep together with those owned by other members of his extended family and tended them all on behalf of the extended family unit.[14]

Jesus' audience would have known that the shepherd was of the peasant class since he brought the sheep home (Luke 15:6). Peasants, living at the edges of uncultivated pasture lands (here called "wilderness" [15:4]), would bring their sheep home in the evening and put them in the family courtyard for the night.[15] Usually a shepherd with one hundred sheep would have a helper so that, in the case of a stray sheep, the assistant could tend the flock while the shepherd looked for the lost one. At the end of the day, the assistant would lead the flock to the home, and the shepherd could bear the lost sheep home.[16]

In the parable, the sheep, grazing in a mountain region, has become separated from the flock. A lost sheep lies down, bleats, and refuses to move. The shepherd, on finding him, has no choice but to lift the sheep up on his shoulders and carry him home. The figure of a shepherd carrying a sheep safely home is a venerable symbol in Hebrew history, in spite of the low estate the shepherd enjoyed at the time of Jesus. God is pictured as the shepherd in Isaiah 40:11 who "will gather the lambs in his arms" and "will carry them in his bosom, and gently lead those that are with young" (cf. also Isa. 49:22). In a Midrash on Exodus 3:1, a rabbinic parable told of Moses tending the flocks for his father-in-law, rescuing a young lamb lost in a ravine and carrying it back on his shoulders. "Then God said, Because you have shown pity in leading back one of a flock belonging to a man, you shall lead my flock, Israel."[17] Furthermore, there is ample precedent for Israel to express their disloyalty to God in the figure of the lost sheep.[18]

The focus of the parable is on the joy that accompanied the finding of one lost sheep, one percent of the entire flock. Both Matthew and Luke report that the shepherd went home rejoicing because of this one lost sheep now found. Furthermore, in Luke he called together friends and neighbors so that they could share his joy. Perhaps among them were members of the shepherd's extended family who owned a part of the flock. They celebrated both the finding of the lost sheep and the fact that the shepherd himself had come safely home. That one sheep now recovered was the focus for the celebration rather than the ninety-nine already safe in the peasant family courtyard.

The telling of the parable began with a question. "What is your judgment?" said Jesus, "Is this not what actually would happen?" Perhaps the answer was so obvious that it was assumed: "Of course, that is the way things happen!"

Well, said Jesus, "there will be more joy in heaven over one sinner who repents than over ninety-nine righteous persons who need no repentance" (Luke 15:7). The glimpse we have of the joy of God's Reign in given to us in curious circumstances. It is a group of peasants — family, friends, and neighbors — celebrating the recovery of one lost sheep. And if we can feel their joy, we have some intimation of the joy of God's Reign when one sinner responds to the open invitation and is recovered by God.[19]

The Parable of the Lost Coin
(Luke 15:8–10)

While his accusers were still trying to digest this quick comparison of the peasant shepherd's joy and the welcome afforded sinners, Jesus threw out another parable: "Or what woman, having ten silver coins, if she loses one coin, does not light a lamp and sweep the house and seek diligently until she finds it?" (Luke 15:8). To lift up a poor woman (apparently her life savings consisted of ten silver coins, each worth less than twenty-five cents) as the model of joy in the Reign of God was no less offensive to the Pharisees than the Parable of the Shepherd. The Pharisees had been asked to put themselves into the place of the shepherd. Now they were simply asked to consider the case of a woman who lost a coin.

What status a woman could claim in the community was claimed only in connection with a male, her father or her husband. A widow was therefore most to be pitied since she had no man through whom to lay claim to any rights. So thoroughly was a woman an outcast in Palestinian culture that to this day in certain conservative circles, a speaker will apologize for uttering the word "woman," if the conversation requires it.[20]

Jesus, who in his ministry talked openly with women, responded to them as they joined other hearers and entered into friendships with them (Luke 10:38–42), now chose the example of a poor woman to provide a comparison to the Reign of God.

The details of the parable were realistic. The woman knew that the coin would be in her home because convention forbade her moving about through the village. Women were supposed to avoid public notice. It was preferable for a woman, particularly an unmarried woman, not to leave her home and thus avoid the sight of all men, though these rules were relaxed in instances when the help of the woman was essential for the husband's profession. Since the woman who lost the coin had not walked far beyond her home, she knew where the coin would be found.[21] She would have needed to light a lamp, even in daytime (Luke 15:8), in order to find the coin. The house would have been dark because the one window of her house would have been small (so that a thief could not enter).[22]

The woman took a broom made of palm leaves and swept the reaches of her small room, hoping that the sound of the coin against the rock or hardened dirt floor would help her to find it. Once again, when the lost was found, there was cause for rejoicing. Like the shepherd, she called together her "friends and neighbors" (Luke 15:9) saying, "Rejoice with me, for I have found the coin which I had lost" (Luke 15:9). That is *of course* the way the poor woman would act; her joy is completely in order. The parable has not debated the Law. Rather, it has presented a situation in which joy is in order and has suggested that, in experiencing her joy, the hearers can glimpse God's Reign breaking in.

In the Parables of the Lost Sheep and the Lost Coin, the question is transferred from Jesus, the tax collectors, and the sinners to the questioners. Here are situations in which joy is clearly in order. Are the Pharisees among those who delight that the lost is now found, or are they to take a position along the sidelines and object to the joy?

In both parables, God's Reign comes to us in an unlikely place. Jesus elsewhere promised that we would encounter him in the person of the hungry, the naked, the lonely and imprisoned. Now it is in the courtyard of a shepherd, with sheep, family, and neighbors gathered together, and in the poor hovel of a Palestinian woman, that he invites his hearers to experience joy. And this joy is likened to that which erupts in heaven when one sinner repents. Who can object when the lost are found?

The Parable of the Prodigal Son
(Luke 15:11–32)

With only the brief transitional phrase, "And he said" (15:11), Luke reports yet another parable told by Jesus for the Pharisees. It is clear at the outset that the story concerns two sons and not merely the prodigal: "there was a man who had two sons..." (15:11). Both sons and their responses are central to the story.

The context of the parable changes to the home of a relatively prosperous farmer and landowner. The younger of his two sons asks for his share of the property (15:12). The father, in an immediate response that must have shocked Jesus' hearers, complies and divides his living between the two sons.

Like many of the other parables that Jesus told, he gave little clue to the motivations of the characters. We are left to determine their motivation by looking at their actions. We are not told why the son wished to have his share of the inheritance immediately. But it is apparent that he was anxious to leave home, for it was "not many days" until he had converted his inheritance into cash (15:13) and gone into another country (one of the adjoining countries along the Eastern Mediterranean). He was evidently single and probably about eighteen or twenty years of age.[23]

The parable doesn't tell us the father's reaction to this request of the younger son. It relates only that he complied with the request. The matter of dividing up an inheritance with the sons of a family while the father was living was not unusual. The laws of disposition provided, according to Deuteronomy 21:15–17, for the first-born to receive twice the portion of other sons. In this case, then, the younger brother would receive one-third of the estate. It is possible that only the disposable property was divided in this manner and that the land itself went solely to the older brother, according to the proscription against selling the land in Leviticus 25:23.[24]

The usual practice provided that, while the ownership to property could be changed from the father to the son while the father was alive, the father retained rights to the rent or produce from the land for as long as he lived. Should the son wish to sell the property, it could legally become the buyer's only upon the death of the father. Similarly, the father could not sell the property (since it was legally his son's); he could only dispose of the *use* of the property during his lifetime. The significant element of the son's request was that he first asked for the division of the property and further requested that he be given right of disposal immediately so that he could pursue an independent life elsewhere.

There is some uncertainty in the minds of students of this parable just what this request implied about the son's relationship to the father. Some have concluded that it was not an extraordinary request at all. The younger son could not inherit the land itself (according to one interpretation) and therefore needed to strike out on his own and make as good a living as possible for himself.[25] According to this interpretation, Jesus' hearers would not have thought the younger son's request to be impertinent. They would have known that, with frequent famines in Palestine, a younger son would have needed to find a place for himself in or near one of the great trading cities of the Eastern Mediterranean.[26] Palestinian Jews in large numbers migrated in this pattern. In fact, it has been estimated that at the time of Jesus more than four million Jews lived in the Mediterranean world beyond Palestine, and no more than five hundred thousand lived within Palestine.[27]

But there is persuasive evidence both within the parable and elsewhere to indicate that the request for the right of immediate disposal was an impertinent and insulting request. While a father frequently would divide his property between his sons before his death, the situation represented in this parable is quite different. Here a son requested from his father while he was in good health the disposition of property that could rightfully be his only upon his father's death. This is unprecedented in Middle Eastern literature.[28] For a Palestinian audience his request carried the clear implication, "Father, I cannot wait for you to die."[29] To make this demand was to treat his father as if he were already dead.[30]

The property, at any rate, was now the younger son's. He was free to convert it into the money and clothes that he would need in his new independent life. The older brother followed the legal practice and stayed on the farm as its titled owner. The father still has the right to the produce of the land, but the land belonged to the older son and would be his completely when his father died. For the time being, as his father is later heard to say to his elder son, all that belonged to the father was really the older son's (15:31).

The younger son's wasteful ways in the far country have been the subject of imaginative interpretation ever since the elder brother uncharitably speculated that he spent the money in living with harlots (15:30). Yet all we are told for certain in the Greek text is that he lived wastefully. The word translated "squandered" could mean literally "scattered to the wind," for it was used by Jesus to describe the process of throwing grain into the air to separate it from the chaff (Matt. 25:14–30). The phrase "loose living" certainly means "living wastefully"; but it may or may not imply that the wastefulness is dissolute or morally corrupt.

What was shortly to happen to the son was so thoroughly degrading that the story does not have to hang upon the exact shading of his wasteful ways. For, after he had "run through" the money, a famine arose in the land, and he was hungry. Anyone who has any food in a land of famine is besieged with persons who must have his or her help in order to survive. The young man was offered a chance to tend pigs, a prospect so disgusting and degrading to any young Jewish man that the owner probably thought it would be turned down outright — famine or no famine. But the young son joined the owner. The desperateness of his condition is shown by the word used to describe that he was "joined to" the owner (15:15). The root of the verb, *kallao*, is *kolla*, or glue. The same word was used by Jesus to describe the close and enduring bonds of marriage (Matt. 19:5). The prodigal son's association with the owner, therefore, was a desperate and clutching relationship because it represented his only hope for survival.

It is scarcely necessary to underline the extremity of the son's position. He was working for one of the heathen and in constant contact with animals that were unclean. He could not observe the Sabbath and was therefore virtually forced to renounce his religion.[31] In becoming a tender of pigs, he would now be considered a Gentile and would now be treated as such by any Jew.

A Talmudic proverb went: "Cursed is the man who tends swine, and the man who teaches his son Greek wisdom!"[32]

The son, of course, had no further claim on his family. He had received all of that to which he was entitled from his father. His older brother owed him nothing. Neither could he expect any help from his fellow townspeople. He would receive nothing but taunts and outrage from them were he to return to his home village. An offense against his father was an outrage against the whole social order of a village. He would be subject even to physical abuse were he to appear there again.[33]

The young man's situation grew so extreme that he would have been glad to cram even the pods of the carob tree that were given to the pigs into his own mouth (15:16). This fodder for domestic animals was eaten by humans only in dire emergency. But even that was denied him. So "he came to himself" (indicating that in his previous conduct he was clearly "beside himself" or "out of his mind," as we would say it) (15:17). He recalled that even those servants on the lowest rung of his father's employ would have something to eat — real food, at that, not those carob pods given to the pigs.

Then, in a masterful example of good storytelling, Jesus reports that the son not only determined at that moment to return to his father, but he lets us hear the son rehearse the entreaty that he will make to his father: "Father, I have sinned against heaven and before you; I am no longer worthy to be called your son; treat me as one of your hired servants" (15:18–19). His admission of guilt and assumption of responsibility is outright. The most formidable aspect of his request is for his father to forsake his pride long enough to admit him into his house again.

The position the son requests is the lowest that he could possibly seek. Standing at the top of the staff of servants was the bondsman (*doulos*), a slave. Despite his servile status, he was regarded as a part of the master's family and had a personal interest in the affairs of the master. Considerable authority was given to him. The servant in the Parable of the Faithful and Wise Servant (Matt. 24:45–51/Luke 12:42–46), as we have seen, was given the full authority of the master while he was gone. Bondservants (*paides*) were one level lower than the bondsman. They were the servants who were abused by the bondsman or estate manager in the parable to which we have just referred.

The lowest category were the hired servants (*misthioi*). They were regarded as outsiders having no access to or interest in the affairs of the family. They worked only when extra help was required and could be dismissed at the pleasure of the master. The hired servant was a free man, but he had no security or rights against his employer. He was regarded as inferior to other servants and subject to their direction. This is the position that the younger son requests for himself.[34]

We, the hearers, know the request that the son is to make of his father. The story builds suspense about the father's response. But "while he was yet at a distance," his father *saw him, had compassion, ran, embraced*, and *kissed him* (15:20, emphasis added). He doesn't even reach home before his father is there to greet him. By going out to greet him at some distance, the father spares his returning son from the taunts, humiliation, and hostility of the villagers[35] and makes it clear that the son is not only accepted but that his return is the occasion for joy.

The father's actions are extreme. Then as now it was a mark of status and honor for a Middle Eastern gentleman to walk in a slow, measured pace. Commenting in the second century before Christ, Ben Serach, a scholarly gentleman living in Jerusalem, says, "A gentleman is known by his walk."[36] It is beneath the dignity of an elderly Jewish landowner, clothed in flowing robes, to run down the road for anyone, much less for a son who has humiliated him.[37]

The son does not fall down on his knees in the dust but is immediately embraced and kissed as an equal. An important cue to the father's attitude toward his son is given in the more literal translation in the King James Version. There it is said that the father "fell on his neck, and kissed him" (15:20). A contemporary translation renders it "He...threw his arms around his neck, and kissed him."[38] Whereas peers could greet one another by a kiss on the cheek, the son or servant would kiss the master of the house on the hand.[39] In Jesus' parable the father took the initiative and treated his son as an equal before a word was uttered. The kiss of itself means the son is forgiven, even as David had kissed Absalom when he was placed before the mercy of David (2 Sam. 14:33).

Only now do we hear the speech that the son has carefully said over and over to himself on his way home: "Father, I have

sinned against heaven and before you; I am no longer worthy to
be called your son" (15:21). But that is only a part of the speech.
The rest is never spoken. Before he can ask for anything he is
offered everything. Ragged, dirty, and emaciated as he is, he is
clothed in royal attire. The father issues orders to the servants:

> Bring quickly the best robe, and put it on him; and put
> a ring on his hand, and shoes on his feet; and bring the
> fatted calf and kill it, and let us eat and make merry; for
> this my son was dead, and is alive again; he was lost, and
> is found. (15:22–24)

In place of a confrontation, the son found a coronation. The son
is now given the ceremonial robe that belonged to his father, the
mark of honor that a king would grant to show his esteem for
a visiting official. The signet ring enabled him once more to
mark documents with his own sign, thus implicitly giving him
authority in the household. The shoes indicated that he was a
free man who no longer needed to go barefoot as a slave would
do.[40]

Finally, in an extravagant act, the father orders that the fatted
calf be slaughtered and cooked for a feast. Only rarely did they
eat meat at all; now, in honor of the son, the calf is prepared and
consumed by feasting from all who are around, since this large
quantity of meat, once cooked, could not be preserved long.[41]
It was food sufficient for all the neighbors.

In the joy that erupts on the son's return, we find the surest
cue about the nature of his leaving. If we are to respect the story
as a work of art alone, we are not permitted to assume that the
father knew anything about the fate of his son. He knew only
that he saw him returning in humiliation and ruin. Yet his very
presence on the road to his father's house was such a contrast
to his leaving that the father could speak of him as having been
lost and dead and then found and alive.

But the parable is not complete without the description of
the older brother's reaction. When he returns from his labors in
the field, he hears the music and dancing that has already begun.
Instead of quickening his pace to join in the celebration, he asks
for an explanation (15:26). The servant simply gives an objective
recital of what had happened. The news of the younger brother's

return and the father's response anger rather than gladden him, and he refuses to go in (15:28). That, in itself, is an affront to the father. For the older son to refuse to join in the party raises this family disagreement into public view. Once again, the father is exposed to humiliation from a son. In Palestinian culture the elder son, whatever his thoughts about his brother, would have been expected *as an act of loyalty to his father* to have participated as joint host (on the farm that was after all his) and later taken up with his father any disagreement that he might have.[42]

The father once again lowers the dignity of his position and goes out to seek a son. The son responds in surly fashion without even addressing him as "Father" (15:29). He speaks of his years of work as servitude, using a word based on *doulos*, "slave." He says that he has not disobeyed any command, yet never has he been given a party of anything like this proportion.

But the son cannot let the matter rest there. He continues: "But when this son of yours came, who has devoured your living with harlots, you killed for him the fatted calf" (15:20). The older son claims no relationship to his brother, referring to him as "this son of yours." The older son doesn't even acknowledge that the younger one has returned; he says he "came" (as if he were an intruder!). Further, he speculates on the kind of life the brother had followed and says something he could not have known to be true: that the son had spent all his money on living with prostitutes.

The father corrects him and responds in tones warmer than saying merely "son." He says, "My son," and assures him that the rules by which they had divided the inheritance still apply. "All that is mine is yours" (15:31). Then he gently corrects the brother for denying relationship to his brother. The father says: "It was fitting to make merry and be glad, for this *your brother* was dead, and is alive; he was lost, and is found" (15:32).

The father has not denied the elder son's faithful service, nor has he revoked any element of his agreement. But he has insisted that "it is fitting" to be glad in the context of this great event in which someone who had been dead to him and lost is now marvelously alive and found.

The elder brother has not fared well in the treatment he has received from biblical interpreters. He is easily scorned. G. B. Caird abandons his usual poise to say to him: "He asked for

nothing, desired nothing, enjoyed nothing."[43] But we are obli-
gated to hear the story as Jesus' hearers, the Pharisees, likely
would have heard it. The elder brother, given his presuppositions (given his "world"), has a case. Something has to be said
for constancy and reliability; the world could not operate for
long without it. The father does not deny the validity of what the
son has stated in their father-son conference out of the house.
Stolid obedience to commandments may not warm the heart,
but given the choice between that and wanton wastefulness and
self-indulgence, few would hesitate long in deciding! Jesus took
care to show the father's affection for the elder son as well as
for the younger. Knowing that the Pharisees would identify with
him, Jesus was required to state the case for the elder brother
strongly if the story were to be convincing to them.

And those who had raised the question about Jesus' feasting
with the sinners were left to put their question beside the parable
they had just heard. The aim of the parable was to provide a
glimpse of the Reign of God whose appearance justified and
demanded unusual actions. Anyone could see how in response
to the father's joy in the return of the prodigal it was fitting to
rejoice. In view of God's Reign then dawning, it was essential
to throw off old restraints and welcome those who were lost and
dead but now alive and restored to the household.

THE JOY OF DISCOVERY

The Parables of the Hidden Treasure and of the Pearl
(Matt. 13:44–46)

The joy of God's Reign is also seen in the Parables of the Hidden
Treasure and the Pearl. One who has been searching suddenly
finds what he has sought.

In both of these parables, Jesus utilizes themes that were
prevalent in folktales of the region. The discovery of a buried
casket of jewels and other treasure was the fond hope of many
a poor person in Palestine. Palestine, placed as it was between
Mesopotamia and Egypt, had been the route for waves of inva-
sions across the centuries. The theme of finding buried treasure
is repeated in many Palestinian stories and indeed is a recurring

feature in the folklore of the world.[44] The most secure way to hide treasure from the threat of war or from plunder by thieves was to bury it. This is precisely what one servant in another parable did with his money when his master gave it to him before leaving on a journey (Matt. 25:25).

The hearers of Jesus' parables would have assumed that the finder was a day laborer working in someone else's field and whose life savings were just enough to purchase the field in which he had stumbled upon buried treasure. Perhaps this laborer had himself heard stories of treasure buried and never found. Now this great discovery was his. So he covered up the treasure again, sold all that he had, and purchased the field.

In the Parable of the Pearl of Great Price, the object found was not the result of sheer luck but of a persistent search. Even though this merchant had searched for pearls and traded them throughout the Mediterranean region, the prospect of happening upon a pearl of great price was the realization of a great dream. It was natural for him, having located this pearl, to sell all these others in order that it might be his.

The accent in these parables is not upon the real estate ethics of the man who bought the field or about the relative value of one pearl against several lesser ones. The glimpse we are given here of God's Reign is from the perspective of the one who finds it — or is found by it. In the context of their joy of discovery, the actions of the laborer and the merchant are fitting and necessary.

In Jesus' appearance, the Reign of God for which the hearers and their ancestors had prayed had come to pass. Those who had been excluded were now said to be the cause of an outbreaking of joy in heaven. Those thought wretched were now blessed. The dead now live; the lost are found! Anyone who is alive to the meaning of the time will abandon the conventional measures that exclude the dispossessed and will join in the joy of God's Reign at hand.

QUESTIONS AND SUGGESTED METHODS

1. List as many groups as you can who are scorned, stereotyped, or otherwise prejudiced against by other groups. Then examine the various reasons, spoken or unspoken, which are used

by others to justify this prejudice. Would any group shock religious people of today as the tax collectors and sinners shocked
religious people in Jesus' time?

2. The parables of the Lost Coin and the Lost Sheep are
set in the context of people at the lowest economic and social
standing. Suggest some illustrations of joy of God's Reign that
would concern people who stand in comparable positions in our
society. What does it tell us about the distinctiveness of the joy of
God's Reign? Is the joy that we experience in life directly related
to the relative comfort in which we live? Without overlooking
the misery and wretchedness of poverty, what joy is available
to the poor and the oppressed that is unknowable to the more
comfortable? Does this teach us anything about the nature of
God's Reign?

3. Write and share your own parable illustrating the joy that
accompanies the entry of sinners into God's Reign. Perhaps you
will want to put one of the three parables about the lost into a
contemporary context.

4. With which character in the Prodigal Son do you identify
most easily? If you were to describe the elder son today, what
characteristics would he have? Would he be highly respected in
your community? What justification did he have for feeling as
he did about his brother?

5. What evidence do you find in yourself of kinship with
the elder brother? At the outbreak of joy, do you customarily
join in the dance or seek an explanation? Do you find yourself
resenting the good fortune that comes to another by sheer grace?
When have you known most clearly the joy coming to one who
has received grace? When have you known most clearly that
you have no independent basis for standing up before life? Put
differently, when has it been clear to you that you stood under
condemnation and yet were forgiven and allowed to live?

6. These parables are aimed by Jesus against those who criticized him for welcoming the disreputable into his fellowship.
Does the church today risk any criticism because it has embraced the disreputable in the name of God's Reign? Where are
there examples of those thought to be irreligious and outcast
entering the Reign of God before the "righteous"?

Notes

1. Eta Linnemann, *Jesus of the Parables* (New York: Harper & Row, 1964), p. 69.

2. Gunther Bornkamm, *Jesus of Nazareth*, trans. Irene and Fraser McLuskey with James M. Robinson (New York: Harper & Row, 1960), p. 79.

3. Cf. Joachim Jeremias, *Jerusalem in the Time of Jesus*, trans. F. H. and C. H. Cave (Philadelphia: Fortress, 1969), pp. 360, 375.

4. Kenneth Ewing Bailey, *Poet and Peasant: A Literary Cultural Approach to the Parables in Luke* (Grand Rapids, Mich.: William B. Eerdmans, 1976), p. 143.

5. D. E. Nineham, *The Gospel of St. Mark* (Baltimore: Penguin Books), p. 99.

6. For this listing, see Joachim Jeremias, *The Parables of Jesus* (New York: Charles Scribner's Sons, 1972), p. 132. See also his *Jerusalem in the Time of Jesus*, pp. 303–312.

7. Norman Perrin, *Rediscovering the Teaching of Jesus* (New York: Harper & Row, 1976), p. 106.

8. Jeremias, *Jerusalem in the Time of Jesus*, p. 305.

9. Ibid., p. 311.

10. Bailey, *Poet and Peasant*, p. 151. See also J. Duncan M. Derrett, *Studies in the New Testament*, vol. 3: *Midrash, Haggadah, and the Character of the Community* (Leiden: E. J. Brill, 1982), p. 63.

11. Ibid., p. 147.

12. Ibid., p. 147, n. 24.

13. Ibid., p. 148.

14. Ibid.

15. Ibid., p. 149.

16. Ibid.

17. C. G. Montefiore, *Rabbinic Literature and Gospel Teaching* (1930), p. 259. Quoted In W. O. E. Oesterley, *Gospel Parables* (London: Society for Promoting Christian Knowledge, 1936), p. 181.

18. See, for example, Psalm 119:176 or Isaiah 53:6. See also Derrett, *Midrash, Haggadah, and the Character of the Community*, pp. 60 ff. The same point is stressed in Robert H. Stein, *An Introduction to the Parables of Jesus* (Philadelphia: Westminster Press, 1981), p. 62. This association adds further legitimacy to Jesus' insistence that the gathering in of those normally known as sinners was the fulfillment rather than the abrogation of God's gracious plan.

19. For an extended discussion of the legal and social backgrounds of the Parable of the Lost Sheep and the Parable of the Lost Coin, see Derrett, *Studies in the New Testament*, vol. 3, pp. 59–84.

20. Bailey, *Poet and Peasant*, p. 158, n. 65.

21. Ibid., p. 157.

22. For these and other details, see Oesterley, *Gospel Parables*, pp. 181ff.

23. Jeremias, *The Parables of Jesus*, p. 129.

24. For this view, see Linnemann, *Jesus of the Parables*, pp. 74–75, and Oesterley, *Gospel Parables*, p. 184. Others hold that the entire property was divided. See Jeremias, *Parables of Jesus*, p. 128.

25. Oesterley, *Gospel Parables*, p. 184.

26. Linnemann, *Jesus of the Parables*, p. 75.

27. Jeremias, *The Parables of Jesus*, p. 129.

28. See Robert H. Stein, *An Introduction to the Parables of Jesus* (Philadelphia: Westminster Press, 1981), p. 119.

29. Bailey, *Poet and Peasant*, p. 169.

30. Bornkamm, *Jesus of Nazareth*, p. 126.

31. Jeremias, *Parables of Jesus*, p. 129.

32. Quoted in W. MacLean Gilmour, "Exegesis for the Gospel According to St. Luke," *The Interpreter's Bible*, vol. 8, George A. Buttrick, ed. (New York: Abingdon-Cokesbury, 1952), p. 272.

33. Bailey, *Poet and Peasant*, p. 181.

34. This summary is based upon Oesterley, *Gospel Parables*, pp. 185–186. Kenneth Bailey believes the hired servant to be of higher standing than this summary would indicate and thinks, in fact, that the son showed by his rehearsed request that he wanted to have the job, live in the village, and return to his father all that he owed (*Poet and Peasant*, pp. 176–177). Yet this contradicts the force of the son's unqualified confession that has just preceded. It also assumes considerable charity on the part of the townspeople, an estimate that Bailey elsewhere does not share (*Poet and Peasant*, p. 181). Finally, it shows that the son apparently has not grown any more realistic under his duress, for the wages of a sporadic day laborer could hardly provide him with a margin in any way commensurate with one-third of a relatively wealthy man's estate!

35. Bailey, *Poet and Peasant*, p. 181.

36. Quoted in Kenneth Bailey, *Through Peasant Eyes: More Lucan Parables, Their Culture and Style* (Grand Rapids: William B. Eerdmans Publishing Company, 1980), p. xv.

37. Jeremias, *Parables of Jesus*, p. 130.

38. Joseph A. Fitzmyer, *The Gospel According to Luke (x–xxiv)*, vol. 25A *The Anchor Bible* (Garden City, N.Y.: Doubleday & Company, Inc., 1985), p. 1082.

39. Bailey, *Through Peasant Eyes*, p. 16.

40. Jeremias, *Parables of Jesus*, p. 130.

41. Ibid.

42. Bailey, *Poet and Peasant*, p. 195.

43. G. B. Caird, *The Gospel of St. Luke* (Baltimore: Penguin Books, 1963), p. 182.

44. See a survey of this theme in John Dominic Crossan, *Finding Is the First Act: Trove Folktales and Jesus' Treasure Parable* (Philadelphia: Fortress Press, 1979).

Chapter 5

God's Reign as Reversal of Conventional Notions

The parables give us glimpses of the drastic reordering of order that takes place in God's Reign. God's forgiveness for the sinner and the sheer extension of God's grace in the affairs of men and women becomes the determinative reality by which people are to be understood. Therefore, there is a shock in recognizing that the conventional measures of righteousness and respectability are likely barriers rather than the indispensable prerequisites for entering the Reign of God.

The parables function not only as stories that may be analyzed and interpreted; they serve also to interpret the one who hears them. When we begin to wrestle seriously with the world of the parables, we discover very quickly that we who sought to interpret become the ones who are interpreted.

The hearer comes to the parable, as to any story, with a "world" intact. That is to say that we bring to the parables a notion of the way things are and where we fit into the universe. We bear certain convictions about our own worth and the considerations upon which that worth is based. Fitted into this "world" are our "work ethic," our estimate of the upright life, our religious practice, our notion of responsibility to family and community, and all those basic postures that help to shape us as individuals and as members of a society.

Simon, a Pharisee and a friend of Jesus, provides an example of one who brought his "world" with him when he confronted

Jesus. He had a firm notion about what a prophetic person should know, as well as about who sinners are and how one should regard them. A woman known as a sinner came to Jesus while Jesus was at Simon's house as a dinner guest. She opened a jar of ointment, wet his feet with her tears, and letting her hair down (a gesture that broke all bounds of propriety for female public behavior), wiped his feet with her hair. Simon, entertaining the possibility that Jesus might be a prophet (he called him "Teacher") raised a question about Jesus' perception. His question was completely consistent with his world. Why, if Jesus were a prophet, he asked, did he not recognize that the one who touched him, coming in off the street to talk with Jesus, was a sinner? Simon assumed that if Jesus had known that she were a sinner, he would have separated himself from her and would have had no more to do with her. All the conventions of the world in which Simon dwelt required that. The burden of proof, according to the question, was upon Jesus.

Jesus did not answer the question. Neither did he deal, in the first instance, with the status of the woman as a sinner. Instead, he reversed the question to Simon himself. "Who will love the creditor more," asked Jesus, "the one who is forgiven $50 or $500?" (Luke 7:36ff.). Now the center of gravity of the whole incident was reversed. Simon faced the question. He made the judgment that is obvious. Then Jesus used this as a chance not to debate Simon's sensitivities on associating with sinners but to draw attention to the great love that the woman had shown in response to forgiveness and to contrast that with the rather perfunctory and minimal greeting that Simon himself had extended. Simon, who had *put* the question, had now *become* the question. And Jesus told the woman that her sins were forgiven and that her faith, her response to the great invitation into God's Reign, had saved her; and she was sent in peace. The parable interpreted Simon.

So the parables frequently interpret us when we pause to consider them well. We come to the parables with our world conveniently in place. We seek from the parables perhaps only an added aura of inspiration or information by which to supplement the stance we already have. We place the burden on the parables. But the parables open us up to a world that, by conventional seeing, we will not see (Matt. 13:13). What stance are we to take before this marvelous new happening? Can we rejoice that the poor and the maimed and the lame are brought into God's great banquet (Matt. 22:1–10)? Can we join in the dancing and feasting to which we are invited by the father when his son comes back home (Luke 15:11–32)? Or are we scandalized at the unshapely and distorted who enter the banquet hall and petulant because our long years of faithful labor have not been rewarded in any way comparable to this recently-returned unfaithful son? It is we who are interpreted by the parables.

In the face of this Reign of God irradiated with the love of God, we, the hearers, are brought to a decision. Can we accept a reversal of some of our notions? Will we cling to the old world in which we have found our supports or join in the great celebration of God's Reign?

WHO IS RIGHTEOUS?

The Parable of the Pharisee and the Publican
(Luke 18:9–14)

Some care is needed if we are to hear the reversal in the Parable of the Pharisee and the Publican, as Jesus' first hearers likely heard it. In the centuries since Jesus spoke it, the two figures of the parable have virtually changed places. We are inclined to look somewhat indulgently on the publican because he recognized his sin and cast himself on the mercy of God. And we are so repelled by the self-righteousness of a certain type of Pharisee that we automatically heap upon him the judgment reserved for those who are arrogant, self-righteous, and condescending. When we figuratively enter the scene in the Temple, therefore, we enter with a predisposition in favor of the publican. That is not the way Jesus' hearers would have reacted. For them, the Pharisee was a righteous person.

While smug self-assurance about oneself and condescension toward others were obvious failings of some of the Pharisees — including the ones to whom this parable was addressed — we are not to assume that they were endemic to all. Persons within the Pharisaic circle itself warned against spiritual pride and judgment of others. One of the sayings of Hillel (c. 20 B.C.) was:

"Keep not aloof from the congregation and trust not in thyself until the day of thy death, and judge not thy fellow until thou art come to his place."[1] While some Pharisees, including the one mentioned in this parable, did err on the side of self-righteousness, people would not automatically have assumed that they would be of such a mind.

Similarly, the publican could not have received a hospitable hearing from those who heard Jesus. Publicans not only co-operated with a foreign occupying power, Rome, but padded their living by defrauding others among their own countrymen. Repentance required that they quit their job as tax collectors and restore all that they had illegally taken plus 20 percent.[2] Since it was unlikely that they could name — let alone re-pay — all those whom they had defrauded, they were treated on the same level as robbers. They had no civil rights. The reversal that is effected by the parable will not be apparent unless we are prepared to hear it with this background in mind.

These two contrasting types of people, then, come to the Temple to pray. The Pharisee prayed a prayer of thanksgiving, one that was probably a familiar one to the Pharisees who heard Jesus tell the parable. The prayer that the Pharisee prayed sounds strikingly similar to one that was written by a rabbi about A.D. 70: "I give thanks before thee O Lord my God and God of my fathers, that thou has appointed my portion with those who sit in the College and the Synagogue, and has not appointed my lot in the theatres and circuses. For I labour and they labour. I am keen and they are keen. I labour to inherit Paradise and they labour to inherit the pit of destruction."[3]

In this parable, the Pharisee, standing alone in the Temple,[4] first enumerates those outright sins that he has avoided; he is not an extortionist or swindler, not an adulterer, and not like the tax collector whom he can see standing in the shadows of the Temple. But then he adds the extra works of righteousness that he regularly fulfills. He fasts twice a week, even though Jews were not required to do so. One fast only was required of the Jew, a fast on the Day of Atonement. Only the strictest of the Pharisees imposed upon themselves the practice of fasting two days per week (Monday and Thursday).[5] Clearly this man was zealous not only to fulfill the Law but to go beyond it. The contrast between him and the publican who was utterly outside the Law was dramatic.

But the Pharisee's diligence went even further. He gave tithes of all that he bought (18:12). Ordinarily, in buying corn, new wine, and oil he could have assumed that a tithe had been paid by the one who had produced it. He, taking no chances, paid his tithe on them as well.[6] The Pharisees who heard the parable would recognize this man to be an unusually diligent and upright man.

The Pharisees likewise would have shuddered at the mention of the tax collector who stood in the shadows of the Temple, daring not to raise his eyes toward heaven. The tax collector, in contrast to the Pharisee, recognized that by any means of reckoning he could not be justified before God. The Pharisee had assumed a standard of measurement of righteousness and considered that by that standard he was justified. By any standard, the publican would be considered a sinner, so his prayer was simply: "God, be merciful to me a sinner" (18:13). And it was he, said Jesus, who went from the Temple on the hill back down to his house as one justified rather than the Pharisee.

The determinative new standard in the Reign of God was no longer the code that the Pharisee had met and exceeded, but the love of God upon which the sinner could cast himself or herself without reservation. The parable interpreted its hearers. The Pharisees, like the Pharisee in the parable, would have had an inner revulsion against the swindler, the tax collector. Yet Jesus said the publican would receive God's justification rather than the one they considered blameless. It was a shocking and radical reversal of every standard of judgment that they knew.

The Parable of the Two Sons
(Matt. 21:28–32)

When Jesus told the Parable of the Two Sons, he was in the Temple talking with the chief priests and elders (21:23ff.). They entered into a dispute about the authority for his teachings. Then he told the Parable of the Two Sons. One son, on being asked by his father to go and work in the vineyard, answered that he would not. But later he repented and went to the vineyard to work. A second son, however, answered immediately that he would go to work in the vineyard, but he did not go. Then Jesus asked them which of the two sons did the will of the Father.

When they answered with the obvious answer, Jesus responded that harlots and tax collectors would enter God's Reign before them; for, while the Pharisees had not believed John when he preached for repentance, the sinners had heard John and repented. Those who hear and repent, even if their first response is disobedient, are closer to God's Reign than those who indicate that they are responding to God but fail to repent and believe.

This is a reversal of dramatic proportion, a direct turn from any known method of reckoning righteousness. Those commonly thought to be sinners are now announced as first in line for God's Reign, even before they show any signs of making restitution for their sins. It is a hint of the nature of God's Reign.

The Parable of the Rich Man and Lazarus
(Luke 16:19–31)

In the Parable of the Rich Man and Lazarus, there is no reason to think that Jesus was seeking to teach the details of life after death. Neither was he simply endorsing the notion that those who are good and those who are wicked receive their just reward in the life to come. Jesus here adapts for his own use a very old story, one version of which came from Egypt. It was told by the rabbis at the time of Jesus.[7] To see more clearly what this parable is teaching, we look at the shape of the story.

The conditions of the two men are contrasted starkly. The rich man was clothed in purple, the clothing associated with royalty, and wore undergarments of fine linen, the most luxurious fabric in the Middle Eastern world. We know that the house in which he lived was large, for it had a gate or porch, which was a measure of a large and expensive home. We are told that the wealthy man enjoyed rich feasts every day. Apparently he not only lived on a grand scale but made this the focus of the life.

Lazarus, the only character in all of Jesus' parables to be given a name, contrasted markedly to the wealthy man at whose gate he begged. Lazarus was hungry and emaciated. He was poorly clothed. The sores that covered his ulcerated skin were exposed. Dogs, unclean animals, licked his sores, and the dispirited Lazarus could not even frighten away the dogs that added to his misery.

Any listener of Jesus' would have assumed that Lazarus was a sinner and that his wretched situation was a punishment from God. Conversely, the rich man who had his ease would be considered a righteous man, else he would not have been so richly favored by wealth. Every detail given in this parable leads one to think that the wealthy man is a Sadducee; they were of the wealthy class, and they, like the rich man, did not believe in the resurrection.

The difference in their fates after death is stark. When Lazarus died, he was carried by angels to "Abraham's bosom." He was, therefore, in the favored position in the eschatological banquet, the heavenly feast in the Age to come. On the other hand, the rich man's punishment was not only to suffer in Hades, thirsting without water to drink and suffering the anguish of flames (16:24), but also to undergo the torment of looking into the distant heaven and seeing the beggar. He pleaded to Abraham to send Lazarus to dip water upon his tongue. Now, even in his desperate straits, he thought of Lazarus as his social inferior. He asked that Lazarus be sent to him just as he was accustomed to summoning servants before his death.

When his petition to Abraham was denied, the rich man asked that Lazarus might be sent on another mission. In this case it was to go to his five brothers who, like him in his former life, did not believe in life after death. They at least should be warned so that they might live the kind of life that would save them from the anguish of Hades.

Even this, however, was denied him, for, said Abraham, "If they do not hear Moses and the prophets, neither will they be convinced if someone should rise from the dead" (16:31). The Sadducees, in distinction from the Pharisees, believed only in the written Scriptures and not in the "tradition of the elders." In this parable, the Sadducees were told that their own authorities were sufficient to warn them against this torment. Here Jesus engages in a satire at the expense of the Sadducees. In effect he was saying, "If they don't understand their duty as their own Bible tells it, they are so dull that even a brother returning from the dead would fail to persuade them!"

Jesus used this parable as a description of God's Reign. In

seeing Lazarus transported to the bosom of Abraham on angels' wings, while the one who withheld crumbs of bread from him pleads for mercy from Hades, we are glimpsing the reversal of conventional notions wrought by the coming Reign of God.

Through this parable Jesus also puts his hearers on alert. Even now in the midst of their daily affairs matters of great moment are at stake. Had the rich man had any clue that his eternal destiny was related to the miserable and presumed sinner Lazarus, he would have conducted himself quite differently. The Reign of God in effect came to the rich man disguised as an ulcerated, homeless victim. And the rich man missed his opportunity. To elect for the Reign of God is to see Lazarus and all other features of our everyday life in a radically new context.

The Parable of the Good Samaritan
(Luke 10:25–37)

Perhaps the most troublesome reversal for Jesus' opponents to accept was one involving the Samaritan who proved to be a neighbor and a model of God's Reign. Luke set this parable in the context of a lawyer's question to Jesus. The lawyer, a scribe and a Pharisee according to Matthew (22:34–35) and Mark (12:28), questioned him about what he must do to inherit eternal life. Jesus responded by putting the question to him: "What is written in the Law?" And the lawyer answered with a recitation of the commandment to love God and neighbor. When Jesus approved his answer and further said, "Do this, and you will live," the lawyer tested Jesus' knowledge of the law by pressing further. He asked, "And who is my neighbor?"

It was not unusual to test the ability of a teacher by putting such questions before him. Nor was the question of mere academic interest. At the time of Jesus, many Gentiles had come into Palestine. There was a question whether the obligations to a neighbor extended to these Romans, Syrians, and Greeks.[8] Many Jews concluded that obligations to neighbors included only other natural Jews or those fully converted to Judaism. Some Pharisees excluded as neighbors those who lived in the towns or rural areas and thus could not learn or keep the full demands of the Law. Quite frequently, individuals excluded their personal enemies from the ranks of those who had a claim upon them as neighbor.[9] The lawyer who was a Pharisee was calculating the limits of the circle to whom he owed love comparable to his love for God and for self.

The question, of course, was not answered. Instead, another question was put to the lawyer. The story concerned a hapless traveler going down from Jerusalem to Jericho, a distance of about seventeen miles. His nationality or religion is not given. The way he traveled was marked by ravines, sharp turns, caves, and other places where thieves could hide. It was a route so dangerous that it was called the "path of blood."[10] The traveler in Jesus' parable was not only robbed but he was stripped of his clothes, beaten, and left "half dead."

Jesus recounted that two Temple officials, a priest and a Levite, passed by. The hierarchy of the Temple included Levites, the lowest order, priests, and the high priests. The parable does not tell us the reasons why the two clergy disregarded the half-dead victim beside the road. Some have speculated that they would not have been allowed to minister to him because, taking him to be dead, their touching him would have compromised the ritual purity demanded of Temple officiaries. Kenneth Bailey, for example, speculates that the priest was one of a number of his profession who served for two weeks in the Temple in Jerusalem and then returned to their homes in Jericho. Since he would have been ceremonially clean, any approach to the wounded man would seriously compromise his standing. Just to see if he were still alive, for example, would make the priest unclean, since any approach to the dead closer than four cubits (about six feet) was considered a defilement. Were he thus defiled he would be subject to embarrassment and humiliation for having contacted uncleanness. Furthermore, he would have been required to undertake an expensive process of purification lasting a full week.[11]

It is thus quite likely that the priest was faced with quite a predicament, given the presuppositions of his religious worldview. The parable does not require, however, that we enter fully into his reasoning. The fact is that the priest and the Levite, persons conventionally thought to be righteous, did not heed the plight of the man who was beaten and left half-dead.

The emotional crux of the parable occurs in verse 33 when

Jesus introduces a Samaritan. The Samaritan came to the victim, saw him, and had compassion upon him. The clerical travelers were not even said to have delayed their journey in the least or to have had any compassion upon him. The Samaritan, however, stopped, bound up his wounds (presumably by tearing cloth from his own garments), cleansing them with oil and wine, set him upon his own beast, and brought him to an inn. The Samaritan, who had been riding, now walked before his beast which carried the injured traveler to the inn. He paid for the immediate cost of nursing the man back to full strength, and he promised to return soon to pay any additional amount that would be required.

The introduction of a Samaritan with compassionate impulses was yet another shock to Jesus' hearers. There was deep and historic enmity between the Jews and the Samaritans. The Jews despised the Samaritans because they had mixed with the heathens who had come into their land. They did not strictly observe the religion of Israel. Disowned as fellow citizens when the Jews returned from exile in 536 B.C., the Samaritans were not allowed to participate in the building of the new Temple. They built their own temple on Mt. Gerizim and had no part in the Temple worship of Jerusalem.

The enmity was so deep that Jews cursed Samaritans publicly in the synagogues and prayed that God would allow them no share in eternal life. The faithful Jews would have no contact with the Samaritan or with anything that the Samaritan had made.[12] The Samaritans bore an equally intense hatred of the Jews, perhaps reflected at its depth in the action of some Samaritans between 9 and 6 B.C. in defiling the Temple area by scattering men's bones over it and thus precluding the possibility of celebrating the Passover.[13]

The New Testament reflects this enmity at many points. Jesus could find no shelter in Samaria because he was going toward the Temple (Luke 9:52–53). The woman at the well in Samaria was astonished that Jesus would ask her for water, "for Jews have no dealings with Samaritans" (John 4:9). Calling a person a Samaritan was equivalent to saying that he or she was demon-possessed (John 8:48).

This, then, is the reversal at work in the parable. The official representatives of the Temple, usually thought righteous, fail the test. And the one who is the model of a neighbor is a member of the hated Samaritans.

The lawyer was so affronted that he could not bear to let the despicable word "Samaritan" cross his lips. When Jesus asked him who of the three proved to be a neighbor to the one in need, he circumvented the word by saying "the one who showed mercy on him." So Jesus said, "Go and do likewise" (10:37).

The reality of God's Reign transcends or contraverts our conventional notions about who the righteous really are. Here we see the most unlikely people actively portrayed as those who are vindicated before God: a tax collector coming down from the Temple, a sick, miserable beggar, and a despised member of a nation of outcasts. If the hearer can find it within himself or herself to grasp the righteousness of these three otherwise contemptible persons, then that person has glimpsed and grasped something of the reversal of God's Reign.

ASTONISHED BY GRACE

The Parable of the Laborers in the Vineyard
(Matt. 20:1–16)

Among all the reversals portrayed in the parables, none does more to interpret the listener than the parable now before us. It provides a glimpse of the grace that is determinative in God's Reign, and in so doing, it portrays the threat that grace represents to our conventional expectations.

The parable would hardly do as a case study in labor relations. An employer went out before 6:00 a.m. to hire laborers. His agreement with them was that they should receive one denarius for a twelve-hour day, a fair wage for a day's work. Then the farmer returned to hire more laborers at 9:00 a.m. His agreement with them on wages was not explicit: "You go into the vineyard too, and whatever is right I will give you" (Matt. 20:4). He repeated the same process at about noon, at 3:00 p.m., and even at 5:00 p.m., one hour before the customary quitting-time.

When it came time to pay the workers for their day, those who had arrived last were paid first. Those who had worked all day and were standing in line to await their pay were astonished to see that those who came only at noon or at 3:00 or at 5:00 were getting a full denarius for their part of the day. They thought that they would receive a proportionately larger amount. But when it came their turn, they received only the denarius that they had been promised. Not unexpectedly they complained to the employer, for those who had arrived last had not only worked a shorter time but they had escaped the heat of the day. The householder heard their complaint but then responded in two ways: (1) "I have paid you," he said, "what we agreed to this morning when I hired you"; and (2) "Furthermore, am I not free to give as I wish of that which is mine?" And then he asked: "Am I not allowed to do what I choose with what belongs to me? Or do you begrudge my generosity?" (Matt. 20:15). The workers' question was redirected. The question was no longer why the employer distributed that which was his as he did; rather the question was why they begrudged him the right to do with his money what he out of sheer goodness chose to do.

We burden the parable unduly if we dwell upon the appropriateness of the employer's wage policy. It was not intended to teach us at this level. Rather, we have here a situation in which sheer incalculable grace is at work.

It was scandalous to the Pharisees when Jesus said that the gathering of the unrighteous was itself a sign of God's Reign. The thought that those who had not engaged in lifelong serious study of the Law could even, at this late hour, walk into God's Reign with those who had labored at it for many years was an offense. It raised radical questions at the very point at which the Pharisees thought they were invulnerable. It challenged a whole system. The world in which they lived, shaped as it was by predictable, measurable rewards, was sundered.[14]

While it was quite natural for the laborers to raise an eyebrow at the generous treatment shown to the latecomers, in the case of the Pharisees it betrayed something fundamental about their stance toward life. Thinking that life could be summed up in commands and their faithfulness to them, they regarded themselves as ones able to justify themselves, capable of standing before life having "paid their dues" and thus deserving a reward dependably delivered.[15] All of life that was novelty and surprise, the gift of grace, was thereby blotted from their sight.

We may understand Jesus' point more clearly when we note the manner in which this same theme was used by others to underline quite a different point. One rabbinical parallel concerned a parable told at the funeral of a distinguished rabbi, Rabbi Bun bar Hijja, who had died at an early age. In this parable, a king, having hired a crew of laborers, noticed that one worker outshone all the rest in his skill and hard work. When they had been working only two hours, he took this laborer and walked with him throughout the day. When it came time to pay the laborers, he gave the one with whom he had walked the same amount as that given to those who had worked all day. When the workers protested, the king replied, "I have not wronged you; this labourer has done more in two hours than you have done during the whole day."[16] The implication was that God had called this young but exceptionally faithful worker to be with him because even in his tender years he had done more than many do in a full lifetime.

Jesus' point is quite different. The rabbinic version does not challenge the notion that certain actions earn certain dependable rewards. The character in the rabbinic version was awarded equal pay not out of grace but out of his exceptionally high productivity. Jesus' parable says nothing about the productivity or industry of those who came later. All that is beside the point. The point is that the employer chose to show goodness toward them.

The one who has committed himself or herself to life in an orderly pattern with obligatory duties and predictable rewards will perceive any disruption of that order not as promise but as threat. That person is like the elder son who, on hearing the sound of music, feasting, and dancing, didn't join the dance but demanded an explanation. Perhaps only those who know that they cannot measure up are prepared to hear of grace as good news. To have faith is to embrace this possibility and to discover grace as hope and vindication for our lives. Those who believe that they have secured the basis for such vindication elsewhere will likely view this as offense and disruption.

ACCUMULATED WEALTH

The Parable of the Rich Fool
(Luke 12:13-21)

The Parable of the Rich Fool is set in the context of a discussion with two brothers concerning the division of their inheritance. Jesus' response was to tell a parable that put accumulated wealth in the perspective of God's Reign. The wealthy farmer in the parable had large holdings of grain from his harvest and wanted only for sufficient storage. He therefore pulled down his old barns and built new, larger ones. Then, he said to himself: "Soul, you have ample goods laid up for many years; take your ease, eat, drink, and be merry" (Luke 12:19). But God said that he was a fool, since that very night his soul would be required of him.

The farmer's being called a fool did not mean merely that he was unintelligent or imprudent. In the biblical sense, it meant someone who by his or her actions denied that God exists.[17] Just as some of those to whom Jesus was speaking had sought to become secure by their moral and religious attainment, so this farmer thought to secure himself from want by the accumulation of wealth. Were he a modern man, he would have spoken of investing enough to assure his continuing prosperity through growth and earnings on his investments. But with a sudden stroke, all his elaborately contrived plans were subverted, and the feasting and drinking that was thought to provide him with joy was denied him. There is the strong suggestion that the rich young man was quite self-absorbed in his aggressive push for more possessions. So isolated was he that there was question about who would inherit his extensive wealth:[18] "And the things you have prepared, whose will they be?" (Luke 12:20). Thus the advent of God's Reign represents a reversal of conventional expectations.

These parables represent a threat for all those who have reduced their world to dependable verities and predictable rewards. Against prevailing notions about who is religious, who merits rewards, and wherein security rests, God's Reign breaks in. To see in that irruption a possibility for one's own life and to stake one's life on that possibility is, in part, what it means to believe in God's Reign. To resent the grace that disrupts and disconfirms one's world is to cling to the old age and whatever security and meaning that person can salvage from it. Those who live in God's Reign are ones who depend upon the grace of God.

QUESTIONS AND SUGGESTED METHODS

1. Jesus spoke of the son who said he would not do his father's will and yet did it anyway and of the son who said he would do it and did not. Can you illustrate these two stances of life through people today? Is it possible to identify people who have not verbally complied with religious expectations but who do the deeds of God in our society? Is it promise or threat that those who do the deeds of God, even without the right verbal response, are the ones who go into heaven before those who are righteous?

2. Abraham tells the rich man that if those who have Moses and the prophets have not heeded their warning, then the voice of one back from the dead would not impress upon them the urgent need to change their manner of life. What evidence or experience is most convincing of the reality of God's Reign? In considering the reality of God's Reign, what is it that makes it most believable for you?

3. If the rich man had been granted his request, what message of warning would he have sent his brothers? Some might compose such a message in the form of a poem, letter, or ballad.

4. It may help people to experience the feelings of the principal characters in the Parable of the Good Samaritan to dramatize a situation in which they themselves come upon a person in need. In one situation, persons were instructed to report promptly to another building on a university campus. There they were told that they would be given a test that was very important. They were asked to get to the other building as promptly as possible. Those who arranged this experiment arranged also for there to be a person lying beside the sidewalk who was not known to any of them and who was obviously very ill. Members of the group were released individually to go to the other building. When they arrived at the other building, they discussed their reaction to the situation and examined how their experience aided their understanding of the reaction of people in the parable. Such a simulation, or a variation of it, might be developed by the group.

5. Another approach to the Parable of the Good Samaritan would be to stage or to role play various contemporary situations in which there was a need that was passed by on the part of the righteous and was heeded by one who was an outcast. Individuals could be interviewed about their actions following the dramatization.

6. We, like Jesus' contemporaries, often have attitudes toward near neighbors different from our attitudes toward those further away (either in distance, social standing, education, or some other measure). Examine individually or in a group the various groups within our society or in other nations who are thought to be less deserving of our neighborly response. What individuals or groups within your community would you be excused by conventional folkways from responding to as a neighbor?

7. The priest and the Levite may have feared that they would be corrupted by touching a dead body lying along the road. Who are those groups of people whom we fear will corrupt us through touch or association? What is it we fear? Are there aspects of the priest and the Levite within us?

8. Arrange for a news reporter to be on hand when the employer pays his employees for their day's work. Interview one of those who went to work early in the morning and another who came only an hour before time to quit. Conclude the interviews with the employer, finding out why he paid his employees as he did. With whom do you identify in this scene?

9. What three examples can you cite in which there are dramatic reversals in who is judged righteous, praiseworthy, heroic, or honorable? Are there personal qualities once thought reprehensible that are now considered the mark of faithfulness and courage? In what way is this comparable to the reversal of God's Reign? In what way is it in contrast to the reversal of God's Reign?

Notes

1. Quoted in T. W. Manson, *The Sayings of Jesus* (London: SCM Press, 1937, 1961), p. 309.

2. Joachim Jeremias, *The Parables of Jesus* (New York: Charles Scribner's Sons, 1972), pp. 141, 143.

3. Rabbi Nechunya b. Ha Kana. Quoted in Manson, *The Sayings of Jesus*, p. 311.

4. Manson, *The Sayings of Jesus*, p. 310.

5. Ibid., p. 311.

6. Jeremias, *The Parables of Jesus*, p. 140.

7. See John Drury, *The Parables in the Gospels: History and Allegory* (London: SPCK, 1985), pp. 150–151.

8. Eta Linnemann, *Jesus of the Parables* (New York: Harper & Row, 1964), p. 52.

9. Ibid.

10. Geraint V. Jones, *The Art and Truth of the Parables* (London: S.P.C.K., 1964), p. 210.

11. For this reason, see Kenneth E. Bailey's *Through Peasant Eyes: More Lucan Parables, Their Culture and Style* (Grand Rapids: William B. Eerdmans Publishing Company, 1980), p. 45.

12. Linnemann, *Jesus of the Parables*, pp. 53–54.

13. Ibid., p. 54.

14. Ibid., p. 86.

15. Dan Otto Via, Jr., *The Parables: Their Literary and Existential Dimension* (Philadelphia: Fortress, 1967), p. 152.

16. Quoted in Jeremias, *The Parables of Jesus*, p. 138. For allusion to additional rabbinic stories employing the same theme, see Drury, *The Parables in the Gospels*, pp. 93 ff.

17. Ibid., p. 165.

18. Bailey, *Through Peasant Eyes*, p. 67.

Chapter 6

The Response Required

The terrible urgency of Jesus' ministry was not to convey new information or to make his hearers better informed. Information, good news, was involved, to be sure. But his basic intent was not to call attention to a new fact here and there. It was to reorient the perspective through which the entire world is perceived. He sought to reorient his hearers through the depiction of a new model of the world. Hence parables were the characteristic way he declared the advent of God's Reign. Just as students of subatomic physics are required to learn new models in order to interpret what they observe, so Jesus provided new models or inclusive metaphors, parables, to reorient those who heard him and invite them willingly to enter God's New Age.[1]

His agenda is clear at the outset of Mark's Gospel: "Repent, and believe in the gospel" (Mark 1:15). Believing in the Gospel required turning away even from livelihood and family and adopting a new life consistent with the demands and promises of God's Reign (Mark 1:17).

Jesus used vivid figures to communicate the dreadful urgency that rested upon the decision for God's Reign. It is as if one were a poor peasant being taken to court in a hopeless case (Matt. 5:25–26/Luke 12:57–59). In such a dire situation, it would be necessary to do anything to come to terms with the adversary lest the case should come into court and the debtor be thrown into prison where he could never earn the money required to pay off his obligations. Even now, said Jesus, judgment was being made, and it was essential that people heed the announcement, repent, and turn to God's Reign.

COUNTING THE COST

The Parables of the Tower Builder
and the King Contemplating a Campaign
(Luke 14:28–32)

The twin parables, the Tower Builder and the King Contemplating a Campaign, articulate the theme of the seriousness of discipleship that is present throughout Jesus' teaching: "Let the one who elects to live in God's Reign take heed," says Jesus. Otherwise he or she will be as ludicrous as the one who starts to build a large building or tower and, having installed an excellent foundation, will not be able to complete the structure. What is more pointless than an elaborate foundation that has nothing to support (Luke 14:28–30)! Well might people have reason to mock such an improvident builder! Again, the forethought necessary is compared to a king going forth to war. He needs to consider whether or not he has any chance of prevailing with the resources at hand, whether his ten thousand can hope to withstand the twenty thousand arrayed against him. If there is no prospect that he can be successful, he should not undertake the campaign in the first place. It would be far better not to begin at all, the parable implies, than to set out as a disciple of God's Reign and then be found wanting the commitment necessary to be faithful to the end. "So, therefore, whoever of you does not renounce all that he has cannot be my disciple" (Luke 14:33).

Discipleship requires renunciation of all else. The verb translated "renounce" means to bid farewell to or to say goodbye to and is so used elsewhere in the New Testament (Mark 6:46; Luke 9:61; Acts 18:18, 21; and 2 Cor. 2:13). Unless one is prepared to entertain such forethought and renunciation, it would be better for her or him not to become a disciple in the first place.

TAKING DRASTIC STEPS

The Parable of the Unjust Steward
(Luke 16:1–8)

One of the most difficult of all the parables is that of the Unjust Steward. One commentator goes so far as to say that "there is nothing edifying about it."[2] Present-day readers are shocked not only because of the chicanery involved but because they interpret the parable to approve of this blatantly dishonest conduct.

The story starts with the familiar rich man and his steward. The steward bears the same title as that borne by a more appealing model for the office in Luke 12:42. He was really the agent or the manager for his master who himself may have lived some distance away. Word got around in the community that this steward was "wasting" his master's goods, and that word eventually came back to the master himself. The verb used for "wasting" or squandering" or "throwing to the wind," *diaskorpidzo*, is the same verb used to describe the younger son's wastefulness in the far country in the Parable of the Prodigal Son that has just preceded this one (cf. Luke 15:13). As we shall see, there are parallels in matters other than vocabulary between these two parables as Luke records them.

The owner calls the agent or the steward before him and presents him with the charges. The steward's silence shows that he does not contest the charge, that he likely recognized his guilt, and that he knows his master too well to attempt any elaborate "explanations."[3] Instead of firing him on the spot and having him thrown into jail, as most of his peers would have done,[4] the master tells him to turn in the books because he is no longer to be his agent. The master shows himself to be unusually merciful.

The reason that most owners would have fired him on the spot quickly becomes apparent. Having entered the pattern of deception, the steward considers his plight to see what approach will deliver him from the bind he is in. He was not strong enough to go into manual work and ashamed to beg (16:3). What he does not say is that he could not expect to enter such a responsible position with another employer since he betrayed his responsibilities with this one.

He considers that his most promising course is to place others in his debt by granting them favors while he can still exercise authority under the master so that when he is out of a job they will "owe him something" (16:4). Quickly summoning those who owe money to his master, he betrays his haste by the absence of any salutation or address. He hurriedly asks each one what he owes the master. The two examples that we are given are not insubstantial amounts. One owes 100 measures of oil, or about 800 gallons, the yield of about 146 olive trees. The other owes the master 100 measures of wheat, more than 27 tons, the amount normally yielded by 100 acres.[5]

Those who owe the wealthy landowner are land renters.[6] The formidable amounts owed will come due at the harvest. The steward quickly gives each one of the debtors the bill and tells him to write 50 and 80 respectively, reducing what they will owe the landowner at harvest time.

There is good reason for the servant's haste in acting. If he were to wait until the news of his dismissal spread, then the debtors could not alter their debts. In that event they would be implicated in the deception and would not have an opportunity to gain the use of the land again. But the wily steward quickly makes arrangements before the debtors know; therefore, they act in good faith and have no way of knowing that the steward no longer has authority to adjust rents.

It takes little imagination to understand the kind of hero that this scoundrel would appear to be to the townspeople. In all likelihood he assured them that he had talked his master into this generous act. Even when they found out that the steward was fired from his job, they likely still would have admired him for tricking the wealthy landowner without implicating them. He might be a scoundrel and a rogue, but he has cleverly made sure he will have some "I.O.U.'s," as we would say, when he no longer has a job.

What was the landowner to do when it became apparent to him that he had been defrauded of rent? Already, on hearing that the loan was forgiven in part, the landowner was becoming a popular figure. His tenants were praising him as a generous and understanding man. He could have gone to those who have had changed their account book and explain that it was all a mistake, immediately cancelling the good will that had so recently been heaped upon him. In doing so, he would have further elevated his dishonest steward as a champion of the people. On the other hand, he could have simply recognized that he had been outmaneuvered and moved to solidify a reputation for being generous and understanding. Any Middle Eastern landowner would take pride in such a reputation.

It was the latter course that he chose. When in verse 8 there is reference to "the master," it is to be understood as the landowner who has already been referred to as "master" in verses 3 and 5 above. The praise of the landowner for his wily (though dishonest) agent, then, was not out of satisfaction with the result of his chicanery but out of grudging recognition of his cleverness in self-preservation. The master knew when he had been outwitted. His steward was a scoundrel — but a clever one. And because he was a merciful man he did not jail the erring steward.[7]

In his case, the steward has not only been clever; he has staked all on the mercy of his master and has found that his confidence has not been misspent. If this interpretation is followed, then there are evident parallels between this parable and the Parable of the Prodigal Son that immediately precedes it. In both cases a trust has been betrayed. In both instances, though with varying motivations, the erring one is received again. In neither case does the offender offer an excuse. Both parables leave the conclusion open ended.

In the parable, Jesus was not lifting up exemplary behavior for managers, any more than his other parables were meant to commend an unjust judge, a friend reluctant to give food at midnight, or a person who bought a piece of property without disclosing the wealth to be found buried on it. He was commending, rather, the action of this scoundrel who recognized the crisis he was in and took resolute action to prepare for it. How much more, then, should those who declare their loyalty to him and to God's Reign be speedy and prudent in preparing for the test that is just ahead when God's Reign comes in power! A quick and prudent response is required.

THE URGENCY OF MAKING A CHOICE

The Parable of the Marriage Feast
(Matt. 22:1–10 / Luke 14:16–24)

When we compare the two versions of the Parable of the Marriage Feast, we notice significant differences between them. The banquet given by "a man" in Luke has become in Matthew a marriage feast given by a king for his son. In place of the one servant reported by Luke to have been sent to spread the word that the banquet is ready, Matthew says that several servants are sent. Luke tells us merely that the host was angry when his servant reported the excuses of those who were not ready to come. Matthew, on the other hand, reports that the king's servants not only heard excuses but were "treated... shamefully, and killed" (Matt. 22:7).

The focus of the parable in Matthew and Luke is the command to go out and invite anyone whom they can find to come to the marriage feast, "both good and bad" (Matt. 22:10), so that the hall can be filled. The reference to the mixed quality of those who came may have reflected the belief that the faithful were to be patient with both good and bad now, since the Lord would separate out the good from the bad when he returned.

The original emphasis as Jesus told it was likely upon the excuses offered by the invited guests and the subsequent invitation to the poor, maimed, blind, and lame (Luke 14:21). This message was designed to disarm the protest by Jesus' adversaries against his invitation to sinners.[8] It also stressed the urgency of responding immediately and decisively to the invitation extended.[9]

We have already noticed the rich significance of the meal as symbol for the hour of salvation. Psalm 23:5 pictures God as host for a meal, and Isaiah 25:6–9 gives further detail for the great feast on the mountaintop that God will provide when the divine salvation is at hand. We need not interpret this parable as an allegory to know that an invitation to a great feast or wedding banquet would convey to Jesus' listeners images of the coming of the Reign of God.

The customs surrounding the banquet were familiar to the people in Jesus' audience. In sending his servant on the day of the banquet, the host was simply following the normal procedure for a wealthy host. The prospective guest was given an invitation and, as a courtesy, was informed of the names of other guests who were also invited.

Furthermore, the number of acceptances from the first invitation provided the host with an indication of the amount of meat that would be required for the banquet. Thus a large animal, or several small ones, would be killed and prepared for a large banquet. A much smaller quantity would suffice for a smaller guest list. Since the food would already have been prepared for those who had accepted, the host understandably will be upset if the meat he has prepared now remains with no one to eat it and no means of preserving it.[10] With these preparations made, the servant was sent to those who had accepted the invitation and asked to tell them that the dinner was ready for them.[11]

With almost incredible uniformity, the prospective guests had excuses to offer the servant when he announced the banquet. One had bought a field; another had bought five yoke of oxen. Yet another had married a wife and, as such, was excused from obligatory attendance at such occasions (Luke 14:18–20). All of them employed excuses that had some religious and cultural support but that moved the host to anger. His anger was understandable. At the least, these last-minute refusals showed a lack of consideration to the host. For example, it is true that one who was recently married was excused from military service for a year (see Deut. 20:7, 24:5), yet the newly-married man (only men would have been invited) would surely have known of his matrimonial plans when he was first invited.[12]

One commentator hears in these excuses not only a quality of readiness but a calculated, fabricated put-down to the host. It would strain the host's credulity, for example, to believe that something as important as land would have been bought sight unseen![13] They are at least saying that they have more important things to do than to come to the party to which they have already accepted an invitation. And in Matthew's account they even "make light" of the invitation itself. We can understand the host's consternation, even if the host's retribution for this insult strikes one as quite an over-reaction! (Matt. 22:7).

Both Matthew and Luke report that when those invited did not come, the host directed the servants to bring in others. Luke says they are to bring in the poor, the maimed, the blind and lame (Luke 14:21). And then he adds the ominous conclusion: "I tell you, none of those men who were invited shall taste my banquet" (Luke 24:24).

The parable contrasts two groups of people, groups into which hearers and readers of the parable today can place themselves. On the one hand there are those who were accustomed to be invited to such occasions. They have little conception of the importance of the invitation and find reasons to "beg off" and even insult the host when the servant of the host comes by. The normal matters of buying and selling occupy them.[14] On the other hand, there are those who are utterly astonished that such an invitation would be extended to them. They are not accustomed to attending such banquets. Therefore, the call to them is an unexpected intrusion of grace.

The Reign of God as it is glimpsed in this parable is a banquet hall crowded with unlikely guests. Those who are ordinarily excluded are present, and those people on everyone's list of invitees are nowhere to be seen. Both groups are taken by surprise. The warning is clear, and Luke's setting for the parable makes it explicit. One of those eating with Jesus rather smugly voiced a pious phrase, "Blessed is he who shall eat bread in the kingdom of God!" (Luke 14:15) The clear implication was that this individual was confident that he or she would be among those dining at the banquet table in the Reign of God. Jesus' story prompts us to be less smug. Those who expect to be there may be absent, and those who have never feasted at banquet tables may be the honored guests. Therefore, it is necessary to respond now.

SHOWING MERCY

The Parable of the Unmerciful Servant
(Matt. 18:24–35)

The parables that we have considered in this chapter have shown that God's Reign requires resourcefulness and prudence. Response to God's Reign also calls for showing mercy to others because those who enter God's Reign do so out of the great mercy that God has shown them. The Parable of the Two Debtors (Luke 7:36–59), as we have already seen, has centered upon this theme.

In the Parable of the Unmerciful Steward, the king has settled accounts with his servants and has called one servant before him who owes him ten thousand talents. The servant is probably a satrap or a provincial ruler. As the story unfolds, it reveals that the king is Gentile.

The debt owed is enormous. A rough equivalent would be ten million dollars. The size of a ten thousand talent debt can be appreciated when we know that Herod the Great had an annual income of nine hundred talents and that the total annual taxes of Galilee and Peraea in 4 B.C. were two hundred talents.[15] Since *murion* ("ten thousand") was the largest figure used in reckoning amounts, this is simply to be interpreted as a stupendous amount, far exceeding what anyone could hope to repay.

The king, seeing the magnitude of the debt, ordered that the servant, his wife, his children, and all that he had be sold. Only a Gentile king could have given such an order. Jewish Law would not have permitted it. But even the sale of the family as slaves was a token repayment. A slave, at that time, would have been sold for a price only of between $2,500 and $10,000.[16]

The servant assumed the posture of a suppliant and begged for mercy from the king, promising (what was obviously impossible) that he would repay the debt. Immediately the king responded with more than the servant had asked. He not only decided not to sell the man and his whole family into slavery; he forgave the enormous debt entirely because he had pity on him (Matt. 18:27). The servant and his family left free and unthreatened.

The one so recently rescued from slavery came upon another provincial ruler who owned him one thousand dollars. The servant thereupon took the liberty that was his under Jewish law and grabbed the debtor by the neck (the verb *pnigo* means that he choked him, v. 28) and demanded that he repay the thousand dollars immediately. The debtor responded almost exactly as the first servant had just responded to the king: "Have patience with me, and I will repay you." The repayment of this sum, though large, was not at all unthinkable. The creditor refused, however, and sent him to prison until the full amount was paid.

Those who observed the happening were outraged and they

reported what had happened to the king. Because the one who had been forgiven such an enormous debt had not himself shown mercy, he was turned over to the torturers (another indication that it was a Gentile king since torture was forbidden by Jewish law) until he could repay. Since repayment was out of the question, his torture was unending.

This parable offers us a clue to the nature of God's Reign by showing us what it is not. It is not a new set of laws. It is rather characteristic responses that are appropriate — indeed, required — in the light of God's Reign. We have seen that in the context of God's Reign, actions that might have seemed extraordinary are of a sudden understood as appropriate. When a great treasure is found, it is fitting to sell everything and invest in one field. When the lost and dead now appear found and living, merriment, and feasting are in order. Similarly, when God's Reign determined by God's forgiveness dawns, then the showing of mercy is not a new commandment but the only fitting response. The Reign of God is an order in which God's forgiveness shapes our dealings with one another. We who have been shown great mercy show that we have caught the vision of God's Reign when we show mercy to others.

SURRENDERING PRETENSION

The Parables of the Choice Places at Table
and the Servant's Wages (Luke 14:7–11; Luke 17:7–10)

Luke has put the Parable of the Choice Places at Table in the context of a dinner that Jesus shared in the house of a ruler who belonged to the Pharisaic party (Luke 14:1). According to Luke, the almost comic care with which the guests placed themselves in the most prestigious places provoked the parable (14:7).

The scene of the parable is a marriage feast, one of the most formal occasions to which any of those hearing Jesus would have been invited. As such a meal, those entitled to the highest rank and honor (based on age or attainment) customarily would arrive last. In this parable we are asked to picture a man of significant standing who comes to the feast before some of those of highest status have arrived and selects for himself one of the choice seats of honor. As the guests file in, the seats below this man fill in. Then, at the last minute, one of the most prestigious guests arrives. Then our friend who had designs on the highest seat of honor is asked by the host to be seated at the one seat still vacant — the seat with the lowest rank! His zeal in getting a place of honor has yielded him the lowest seat in the house!

The focus of the parable is neither sage advice on etiquette nor prudent counsel for getting the highest honor at the banquet. The focus of Jesus' parable is on appropriate responses to the dawning of God's Reign. In the light of God's eschatological activity, carefully contrived rankings and distinctions of honor are undermined and overthrown (compare Luke 14:11 with Luke 18:14 and Matt. 23:12). Those who depend upon such things as social rank and status (one might add titles, degrees, and possessions to the list) to assure their standing and who carefully cultivate and manipulate that standing will find that, in God's Reign, matters of rank are turned upside down. It is those who have no claim on the existing order who are entering God's Reign; it is those who cling so desperately to the old order who are closed to God's Reign and are thus destined to be humbled.

The consequence of the parable is not to encourage self-effacing humility that seems to regard oneself as of no worth. That may be a strangely inverted quest for a certain kind of standing — as if one could earn merit by being more humble than anyone else! The abandonment of pretension of which Jesus is speaking here and elsewhere comes from a glimpse of God's Reign in which those who were thought utterly wretched, irreligious, miserable and abandoned now sit at table in places of honor and those who were thought to have a monopoly on matters of place and prerogative, having scorned the invitation, now stand without. In the context of the great reversal that is wrought by God's Reign, the serious scrambling and scheming for a share of prestige and status is worse than pointless; it is comic.[17]

Society's scheme of honors and reputation is now questioned by Jesus: "For every one who exalts himself will be humbled, and he who humbles himself will be exalted" (Luke 14:11). Far better, says Jesus, when making out a list of persons to invite for a dinner, to spurn the first thought of inviting those who can reciprocate with an invitation in kind.

We are bid, then, to have a certain tentativeness about our standing, for it is assured in firmer places! We are invited to entertain a certain nonchalance or abandon about our standing, even as Jesus showed about his, because we have been given to see — even in a glimpse — that our standing has been assured in the heavenly places by an overwhelming "yes" pronounced upon us by God out of the divine grace alone.

For that reason, we are not to keep an account of our merits before God — as if we could accumulate reserves of extra merit that would obligate God to us! When the servant has prepared and served a meal to the master (See the Parable of the Servant's Wages, Luke 17:7–10), that in itself is not remarkable or heroic service. It is simply his task. So in a similar way, the citizen of God's Reign will know that in the light of God's unprecedented outpouring of grace, nothing beside that is a mark of attainment; least of all is it a claim against God.

> So you also, when you have done all that is commanded you, say, "we are unworthy servants; we have only done what was our duty." (Luke 17:10)

QUESTIONS AND SUGGESTED METHODS

1. In the Parables of the Tower Builder and the King Contemplating a Campaign, Jesus speaks of the cost of joining God's Reign. From your understanding of our situation today, what costs are entailed today in declaring allegiance to God's Reign? What elements of one's life are affirmed and strengthened? What elements are denied? In what context does the Reign of God most clearly appear to you? What is the single greatest cost that would be involved in becoming a part of God's Reign?

2. One form of humor is the case of a pretentious person whose efforts to gain attention and acclaim are frustrated. Jesus' Parable of the Choice Places at Table used this form of humor. If you were to tell a parable with the same point today, what situations would you employ? What problems of spirit are disclosed in one's craving for public recognition? Is all aspiration for accomplishment precluded by allegiance to God's Reign? In what manner does God's Reign address the question of status and rank?

3. What factors in the interaction of God's Reign and our own time contribute to the urgency of a decision for God's Reign? How has the urgent need for decision for God's Reign been portrayed in the past? What elements of this appeal are pertinent today? What elements of urgency do you experience in relationship to God's Reign?

4. The Parable of the Marriage Feast lists culturally sanctioned excuses that people offered for not responding. The folkways of that culture provided means of avoiding a choice for God's Reign. Are there prevailing assumptions and patterns in our own culture that help to protect a person from responding to the Gospel? List the excuses given in the accounts of the parable in Matthew and Luke. What excuses would Jesus likely have selected from our own culture? List the ways they are expressed.

5. The early church applied the Parable of the Marriage Feast to its own missionary and evangelistic situation. They were enjoined to invite the poor, the maimed, the blind and the lame. Recognizing that these were the people on the margin of their society, often thought to be in their position because of their sin or someone else's, who are their counterparts today? Just as the early church interpreted this parable in the light of their own situation, how should it be interpreted for our own? If you were to rewrite the parable for today's church and today's evangelistic situation, what features would you include? What are the barriers against the church responding to this responsibility?

6. The Parable of the Unjust Steward reported an incident that would have been of wide interest in the village in which it took place. Arrange for an anchor person and three or four reporters who interpret the parable through news reports and interviews. Reporters can do "live" interviews or use audio or video tape. This parable could also be reported in a newspaper format, using reports on interviews to supplement the main news story. A task force could be assigned to work on this project before the group as a whole has studied the parable. Their reporting could be an introduction to the parable for the entire group.

Notes

1. For this observation I am indebted to Frederick H. Borsch, *Many Things in Parables* (Philadelphia: Fortress Press, 1988), p. 13.

2. W. MacLean Gilmour, "Exegesis for the Gospel According to St. Luke," *The Interpreter's Bible*, vol. 8, George A. Buttrick, ed. (New York: Abingdon-Cokesbury, 1952), p. 280.

3. Kenneth Ewing Bailey, *Poet and Peasant: A Literary Cultural Approach to the Parables in Luke* (Grand Rapids, Mich.: William B. Eerdmans, 1976), p. 97.

4. Ibid., pp. 96, 98.

5. Joachim Jeremias, *Parables of Jesus* (New York: Charles Scribner's Sons, 1972), p. 181.

6. Bailey, *Poet and Peasant*, p. 93. For discussion of economic and social background of the loans, see J. Duncan M. Derrett, *Studies in the New Testament*, vol. 1: *Glimpses of the Legal and Social Presuppositions of the Authors* (Leiden: E. J. Brill, 1977), pp. 1–3.

7. This interpretation is based on findings of Bailey, *Poet and Peasant*, pp. 96–107.

8. Jeremias, *Parables of Jesus*, pp. 63–65.

9. John Drury believes that this parable as it is presented by Matthew can be understood only in the light of the Parable of the Wicked Tenants (Matt. 20:33–41), which immediately precedes it. Both parables, he contends, are dealing with the refusal of Jewish authorities to heed God's entreaties offered through the prophets and finally through Jesus, and the consequent replacement of Judaism by Christianity as the agent of God's Reign (*The Parables in the Gospels*, p. 97).

10. For this background see Bailey, *Through Peasant Eyes*, p. 94.

11. Jeremias, *Jerusalem in the Time of Jesus*, trans. F. H. and C. H. Cave (Philadelphia: Fortress, 1969), p. 93.

12. Bailey, *Through Peasant Eyes*, pp. 98–100.

13. Ibid., pp. 95–97

14. For this emphasis, see Robert W. Funk, *Language, Hermeneutic, and Word of God* (New York: Harper & Row, 1966), pp. 191–192.

15. Eta Linnemann, *Jesus of the Parables*, trans. John Sturdy (New York: Harper & Row, 1964), p. 108.

16. Jeremias, *Parables of Jesus*, p. 211.

17. John Dominic Crossan, *In Parables: The Challenge of the Historical Jesus* (New York: Harper & Row, 1973), p. 70.

Chapter 7

Assurance of God's Reign

In some of the previous chapters of this study, we have referred to the emphasis within the parables upon the triumphant quality of God's Reign. We have spoken of the sudden way in which it intrudes upon the present and about the joy that accompanies its coming. We have referred to the promise of God's Reign as the great affirmation of the disinherited and dispossessed, as well as a threat to those who had become comfortable with this world.

But what of the foreboding signs of resistance that made any talk about God's Reign seem quite unlikely and removed? What had the Gospel to say to those who staked everything on God's New Age and yet suffered so relentlessly from the constraints of the old?

THE MIRACLE OF THE APPEARANCE
OF GOD'S REIGN

One cluster of parables concerns itself with the miraculous manner in which out of small beginnings God's Reign brings forth a glorious result. The familiar imagery of the harvest is used in all but one of these parables, suggesting that the miracle of growth is taking place. Under God's power, the seed of God's Reign that is now working secretly one day will be manifest to all.

The Parable of the Sower
(Matt. 13:3-8 / Mark 4:3-8 / Luke 8:5-8)

The Parable of the Sower illustrates the confidence that should be placed in the coming of God's Reign. As the seed miraculously thrusts forth a bountiful harvest in spite of all the restraining and inhibiting forces, so God's Reign will come suddenly in spite of all that holds it back. Even now the mysterious work of God is going on. It will result in the harvest of God's Reign.

The farming procedures described are faithful to the manner in which a Palestinian farmer would have gone about the work. In Palestine the grain was harvested in June, and the field was left until the sowing time of November or December. The field might be plowed after the harvest, but it was not plowed again before the new crop was sowed.[1] Thus the sower who "went out to sow" was walking across stubble and various thistles that had grown in the field after the last harvest. The seed was broadcast from a cloth that was fastened around the farmer's waist. After a strip of the field was covered with the seed in this broadcast method, it was plowed quickly so that the birds would not consume the bulk of the seed.

It is understandable and logical, therefore, that some of the seed would fall upon the footpath that had been formed by those who had walked through the field. The seed was cast upon the path later to be plowed. Other seed was consumed by the birds. Yet other seed fell upon soil that concealed limestone that lay shallowly under the surface. That seed germinated quickly since the sun warmed the shallow soil and the germinating plant could grow only up. But lacking an adequate root system, it withered quickly under the blistering heat of the sun. The seeds that fell among thistles (or among the seeds of thistles that would grow quickly) were naturally robbed of light and moisture and yielded nothing, if indeed they could grow at all. But, with all this discouragement, there was that seed that fell upon good soil, and the harvest to be reaped from that seed was astounding. A tenfold harvest was good. This seed would yield thirty, sixty, or even a hundredfold. The parable closes with a familiar command that could be translated, "Ye who have ears, prepare to use them now."[2]

All three of the first three evangelists record this parable.

The message seems straightforward. There follow in the Gospel accounts, however, some words that have long puzzled students of the Bible. For Jesus said to his disciples alone:

> To you has been given the secret of the kingdom of God, but for those outside everything is in parables; so that they may indeed see but not perceive, and may indeed hear but not understand; lest they should turn again, and be forgiven. (Mark 4:11–12/Matt. 13:11–14/Luke 8:10)

The principal difficulty in this passage appears at the beginning of Mark 4:12. There, as the passage from Isaiah 6:9 is quoted by Mark, it appears that the parables are given to those outside God's Reign *for the purpose* of obscuring its meaning and of closing them off from the divine forgiveness. This interpretation, of course, violates all that we know elsewhere of Jesus' teaching through the parables.

A number of students of the New Testament have followed the lead of T. W. Manson in interpreting the language of this passage. Manson argues against the notion that Jesus intended the parables to confuse his hearers. He reasons that if Mark were indeed attempting to show that Jesus used the parables in order to bar people from God's Reign, he would not have deleted, as he did, any reference to the one passage (Isa. 6:10) that states that view most explicitly:

> Make the heart of this people fat,
> and their ears heavy,
> and shut their ears,
> and understand with their hearts,
> and turn and be healed.[3]

Manson further notes that Mark is quoting from the Targum (a translation of the Hebrew Scriptures into Aramaic) and not directly from the Hebrew Scriptures. In the original Hebrew, the meaning more likely intended by Jesus in his quotation from Isaiah 6:9f. was as follows:

> To you has God given the secret of the Kingdom of God;
> but to those who are without everything is obscure, in order

that they (as it is written) may "see and yet not see, may hear and yet not understand, unless they turn and God will forgive them."[4]

Such an interpretation is thoroughly consistent with Jesus' use of the parables throughout the first three Gospels.

All three Gospels then follow these words about the use of parables with an explanation by Jesus of the Parable of the Sower that had gone just before. Only in this instance (Matt. 13:18–23/Mark 4:13–20/Luke 8:11–15) and in the Parable of the Weeds (see Matt. 13:36–43) do the Gospel writers report Jesus interpreting his own parables.

On linguistic grounds alone, there are strong grounds for believing that the interpretation of the parable represents not Jesus' teaching itself but rather the effort of early Christians to apply his teaching to their own situation. Words are used in this passage that appear nowhere else in Jesus' teaching but that were prevalent in the early preaching of the church. The manner in which references to preaching are made likewise reflects the situation in the early church more than the context of Jesus' own ministry. These and other powerful considerations make it difficult to believe that this interpretation comes directly from Jesus' teaching.[5]

Other considerations also help us to put this seemingly contradictory statement in context. The word "parables" here refers to a wide variety of sayings from the Hebrew Bible, where in Hebrew the term used is *masal*. The *masal*, translated into Greek as our word "parable," really connoted a whole variety of clothed or enigmatic sayings. At times it is a byword or a proverb. A *masal* can even be a taunt, a blessing, or a curse. Yet other instances of the *masal* are wisdom sayings or riddles.[6] Indeed, *masal* could refer to any "unusual or striking speech."[7] Recognizing this, the words attributed to Jesus have been paraphrased by one commentator: "To you the secret is revealed; those outside are confronted by riddles!"[8]

Beyond these considerations, however, we should understand that in this parable and its subsequent interpretations, particularly Mark's version of it, we are coming face to face with the mystery of the Reign of God itself and the parables with which Jesus announced it. There is something in the nature of the parables that both conceals and reveals. There is a double reference in the parable. It speaks of bread, sheep, wineskins, and seed. At the same time its implicit reference is to something quite other. To those who have entered God's Reign, the parable clarifies what could never be explained by other language. To those who cannot or will not understand, it is a riddle.[9]

The parables, therefore, have decidedly different meanings to those who know the "secret [mystery] of the Kingdom of God" then they do to "those outside." Once again, humor provides an illuminating parallel. Humor frequently communicates to a group sharing similar experiences far better than other means of communication. But to those who do not understand, the laughter that erupts from others is a riddle or a mystery. Jesus' parables sometimes concealed the mystery or secret of the Reign of God. At other times — and there are several — even Jesus' opponents knew exactly what the parable meant (see, for example, Mark 12:12).

Mark especially struggled with the question of why some people rejected Jesus' message. In this section he seems to be saying — in terms more distinct than either Matthew or Luke — that if some do not believe in Jesus it must be because God has willed it so. His partial quotation from Isaiah conveys the notion that for reasons hidden in the divine will God purposes that some should believe and some should not (Mark 4:12).

Boucher has suggested that the "secret" (literally, "mystery") of Mark 4:11 is not merely the identity of Jesus as the Messiah but the nature of the suffering and sacrifice necessary for God's Reign to appear.[10] The nature of this suffering (e.g., the disintegration of the seed) is veiled in parables in the first half of the Gospel. Following Peter's confession, however (Mark 8:29), Jesus speaks forthrightly about the necessity of suffering.

The net effect of the interpretation of the parable in Mark 4:10–12 (Matt. 13:10–15/Luke 8:9–10), however puzzling it may be on first reading, is consistent with the assurance it seeks to provide. In effect it assures those who have said "yes" to the Reign of God and have experienced the mystery of its coming that, despite the suffering and the apparent costly self-expenditure required, the end result is far out of proportion to the modest beginnings of God's Reign. As if to underline this point, Mark repeats essentially the same parable a few lines later (4:26–29) and pointedly notes, as we shall see, that the farmer doesn't agonize over the seed now sown. He sleeps and rises night and day (4:27) and the seed sprouts and grows "of itself" (4:28). There are similar grounds for poise and assurance that God's Reign will unfold in measures we could not have imagined.

Since the parable we are now considering includes an interpretation attributed to Jesus, some comment should be made at this point about the allegorical form that this interpretation takes. Allegories are symbolic stories depicting fictional characters and actions that stand for a truth in quite a different realm. Whereas in a parable there is usually one major point, the force of which we feel as we enter into the parable, in an allegory each detail of the story represents something else. Here in this allegorical interpretation, each of the elements of the story, the seed, the rocky soil, the birds, the sun, and the rest, all these represent something else quite foreign to the setting of the story itself. In a parable, the force of the story depends upon the credibility of what is found in the story itself. Even such extraordinary acts as the father welcoming the prodigal were believable acts, and it was just this credibility that carried the force of the argument.

The principal feature of an allegory that we should note at this point is that it is intended for those who are on the inside. It is really code language in which our comprehension of the story depends upon knowing the code that tells us what each element stands for. By contrast, the parable itself is a means of communication that requires no such inside code.

Throughout Christian history, interpreters have frequently assumed that each parable is really an allegory; and they have consequently pondered their meaning to find hidden (and sometimes quite fanciful) meanings in each detail.[11] The approach taken in this study is that while we should not arbitrarily rule out allegorical elements in the parables, their primary significance is to be found in the action of the story itself understood within the context of Jesus' ministry.[12]

The Parable of the Seed Growing Secretly
(Mark 4:26–29)

The parable that follows in Mark's account is the only parable reported by Mark not also reported by one of the other evangelist. It likewise underlines the assurance that one may have in the coming harvest, or the fulfillment of God's Reign. In this parable the various stages of growth are listed (Mark 4:28). As soon as the grain has ripened, the sickle is put to it "because the harvest has come" (4:29).

That the flowering of God's Reign is the work of God is made clear by the description of the growing process. The farmer scatters seed upon the ground (Mark 4:26), but then he goes about his normal life, sleeping and rising night and day. "The earth produces of itself" (automatically) in an orderly process. The blade appears. Then comes the ear and the full grain in the ear. Then, when these processes are complete, the harvest is at hand (cf. Joel 3:13).

Our notion of plant growth is one of continuity and process in which each stage yields to the next. But it is not continuity alone that is emphasized here; it is also contrast. There is a contrast between the seed as it is cast upon the earth and the subsequent appearance of blade, ear, and grain. The seed is frail, vulnerable, and insignificant when compared to the harvest.

When the seed is scattered, there are two worlds at work. One is the world of the presently-realized, the tangible, the demonstrable. The farmer, in casting the seeds, enters another world. He relies upon the generative power of sun and soil. At the harvest, the world into which the farmer's faith was put comes into glorious fruition.

For those who were discouraged by the uncertainty of the Reign of God, this parable and those clustered about it offered a fortifying glimpse at what was happening. Who could believe in God's Reign on the basis of the tangible evidence? But God's hand is found in the movement of history, as well as in the recesses of the soil. God has planted the seed. The stages of its mysterious growth have taken place. There was basis for assurance, then, in spite of all the evidence to the contrary. The requirement of the situation was to cast one's full reliance upon the mystery of God's Reign and to know that the harvest, while not now at hand, would soon be fulfilled.

The Parable of the Weeds
(Matt. 13:24–30)

Perhaps because of the testing of this faith, a number of other parables with the same theme as the Seed Growing Secretly are recorded in the first three Gospels. Matthew includes a parable that may be an elaboration on the Seed Growing Secretly.[13]

The situation described by the Parable of the Weeds was not an unusual one. The weeds referred to in Matthew's parable are likely darnel. Darnel is a poisonous weed. It is closely related to and, in its earliest stages of growth, is hard to distinguish from wheat.[14] As the crop grows, it is impossible to separate the darnel from the wheat. The roots of the two plants are so intertwined that to pull the darnel would also uproot the wheat.[15]

The situation in which an enemy plants this weed among the good seed apparently was familiar to Jesus' listeners. The act of sowing weeds in a field was enough of a problem to be addressed by Roman law. In some parts of the modern world, it is still used as a threat over one's enemies.[16]

The point of the parable is that, at the present time, the good seed and the darnel are allowed to grow together. But at the time of the harvest, the darnel — at last distinguishable from the wheat — will be bound into separate bundles and used for fuel, while the wheat will be gathered for the harvest.

This parable anticipates the theme of judgment that we are to study later in this chapter. But, at the same time, it conveys assurance to those who observe that the signs of God's Reign are never pure and unambiguous. The parable suggests why good and the evil are for the present allowed to flourish together. At the same time, it promises that a distinction is to be made and the fruits of the good seed will be separated from the evil.

The Parable of the Mustard Seed
(Mark 4:30–32 / Matt. 13:31–32 / Luke 13:18–19)

Yet another parable involving seed and the consequent assurance of the appearance of God's Reign is the Parable of the

Mustard Seed. Once again there is continuity between a seed and the appearance of its full flower. But the stress here is more upon the contrast than upon continuity.

While there are seeds smaller than the mustard seed (cf. Mark 4:31), the mustard seed in Jewish folklore represents the proverbially small — a minute quantity. The contrast between this small beginning and its final result is apparent, since the mustard seed grows into a bush from eight to twelve feet high.[17] The black grains of mustard growing in the pods borne by the mustard tree attract birds to its branches, even though birds ordinarily do not nest in them.[18] The "birds of the air" (Matt. 13:32/Mark 4:32/Luke 13:19) in apocalyptic and rabbinical literature frequently represent the Gentile nations that are to be gathered into God's Reign when it appears.[19]

If the mustard tree contrasts dramatically with its humble beginnings as the proverbially smallest seed of all, how much more will God's Reign contrast with the modest beginnings that now can be observed. Therefore, we are urged to be assured and not to be discouraged by the tenuousness of the seeds of God's Reign that now are visible.

The Parable of the Leaven
(Matt. 13:33 / Luke 13:20–21)

Jesus used the experience of a woman baking her bread to show yet another glimpse of God's Reign. The Parable of the Leaven emphasizes the manner in which God's Reign, though humble and fragile in its beginnings, interpenetrates and permeates the whole and dramatically transforms it.

Just as the seed is hidden in the ground, so the comparatively small measure of leaven is hidden in the dough, an amount equivalent to a bushel.[20] The dough is placed in a container to leaven. And when the baker returns she finds that the formerly inert mass has been transformed. It now has expanded far beyond its former size. It is alive, bubbling with vitality. A small amount of leavening has transformed a large mass of dough. The miracle is in the contrast between the humble nature of its beginnings and the magnitude of its result. So it is with God's Reign. And in that there are grounds for assurance.

GOD'S READINESS TO BRING IN GOD'S REIGN

The basis for assurance in the coming of God's Reign rests in one's confidence in God, for its coming is a gift of God. In two parables recorded by Luke, Jesus speaks of God's readiness to bring in God's Reign by suggesting analogies to human responses in two illustrative situations.

The Parable of the Friend at Midnight
(Luke 11:5–8)

In this parable, a traveler has arrived at a friend's house late in the evening. Travelers often journeyed in the evening by moonlight in order to avoid the heat of the sun. This traveler found his host without bread. That is to say that the host had no unbroken loaves of bread left to offer his guest. It would have been an insult to offer him a loaf that was already broken.[21] A part of gracious hospitality in a Middle Eastern village is to assure a guest that the best food available in that home is really not adequate or fitting for such a distinguished guest. "When a host is being complimented on his meal he will try to turn the compliment by remarking, "This meal is nothing but bread and salt." He means, "Before you, my noble guests, the best I have to offer is only your ordinary fare, indeed, only as bread and salt. You deserve far better."[22]

The host in the parable obviously has recognized his responsibility to feed his guest and refresh him from his journey. He also has recognized that the entertainment of the journeying guest is not solely an individual responsibility; it is a communal one. A guest of one family is the guest of the whole community. On entering a home in present-day Palestine, a guest will sometimes be told not merely that the family is honored at his or her presence but, "You have honored our village."[23]

The host in the parable starts out in the middle of the night to find bread from another household that, as a part of the community, shares the responsibility of providing for the traveler. Since the baking of bread was a communal effort, women who had baked at the village oven knew who in the village had recently baked an ample supply of bread. After a hasty conference in the host family therefore, the host sets out to call for help from a family whom he knows has a sufficient supply on hand.

Jesus asks each of his hearers to put himself or herself into the position of the one who is asked to provide the bread. It is clear from the context and from our understanding of Middle Eastern culture that Jesus expected that anyone should be ready to say yes to the request. The positive answer would be expected because what is at stake is the honor of the friend who has received travelers into his home in the middle of the night. A cardinal principle of friendship is the defense of the friend's honor. His honor and prestige are worth far more to him, in the Middle Eastern setting, than any amount of money. One student of Middle Eastern culture has suggested that inability to defend one's self-respect by providing hospitality could lead the friend to commit suicide.[24] In short, in the situation Jesus has described, it is unthinkable that the friend's request would be denied.

Yet the host runs into reluctance on the part of his friend. Awakened in the middle of the night, the householder calls back to his friend (omitting the title of courtesy that his friend had used in calling, v. 5): "Do not bother me." He continues by telling him that his children are in bed with him and that he cannot (read "does not want to") get up and get him bread. In the one-room Palestinian village, the family would be sleeping together on a raised mat, so that getting up and walking over the children, unbolting the door, and getting the food would be a burdensome undertaking.[25]

If the householder were to refuse such a simple request, the story of his stinginess would be told throughout the village by the break of the next day. And he would be greeted by cries of "shame" wherever he went.[26]

> I tell you, though he will not get up and give him anything because he is his friend, yet because of his importunity he will rise and give him whatever he needs. (Luke 11:8)

Whatever his inconvenience, the householder's sense of honor requires that he grant the request.[27] How much more will God grant God's Reign to those who seek it! There is a further shading to this story that is hard for us to hear in our culture, and it is crucial for understanding the approach to prayer Jesus here is suggesting. The quality of importunity is sometimes interpreted to mean sheer stubborn persistence in approaching God in prayer.[28]

Persistence is involved, but the studies of J. Duncan M. Derrett have revealed another far more subtle dimension to be found here.[29] "*Anidea*," the Greek word in question in this parable, is usually translated as "importunity," but it can also mean "shamelessness" (the New English Bible has used this word in v. 8). Derrett's studies of Greek writings contemporary with Luke's Gospel indicate that this word had come to mean "boldly, without fear of objections." It can mean "without hesitation," with bold faith (cf. James' injunction to pray in confidence, 1:5–8).

The suggestion by Derrett, based on Middle Eastern folkways, is that friends are bold to make claims on one another. Friendship instills confidence that even very demanding requests will be heeded and need not be made with apology or reluctance. Thus friends make known to one another boldly what they need, and they do so without shame, knowing that they will be given what they need.

We need to remember here that the parable is a story and not a proposition. It seeks to establish one principal point, and that is our confidence in praying. The story begins to unravel if we translate it into an allegory and interpret it as a doctrine of God. The Palestinian audience would have known that the direct and bold way the friend asked for bread in the middle of the night was assuredly a request that would be granted, no matter what the inconvenience. The parable is not teaching us that God is irritated at our requests and reluctant to grant what we ask, moved only by our persistence. Quite to the contrary, it enjoins us to ask God for what we need without apology, boldly. It is God's nature to respond to our prayer and unthinkable that our prayer will not be answered.

The Parable of the Unjust Judge
(Luke 18:1–8)

The Parable of the Unjust Judge is clearly matched with the one that just has been discussed. In this parable, Jesus selects a widow as the model of action. This widow, as any other widow in Jesus' time, had no one to intercede for her in the decisions of the judge. She was so poor that she had no money by which to bribe him.

The question of bribery is not out of place in this parable, for this judge was one who, by his own admission, had no fear of God and no regard for other people (the word could mean "reverence for" or "respect for"). The Hebrew who heard this description would understand that the lack of fear for God naturally entailed lack of respect for or regard for human beings, since the two were closely related throughout Hebrew history. The judge in Israel was expected not merely to be an unbiased umpire but a defender for those who had no other defender, to be the champion for the oppressed. The oppressed were the widow, orphan, the poor, and the foreigner. Because Yahweh was the One who cared especially for the victims of persecution, it was necessary for any judge to see that the rights of the powerless were heard.[30] This judge, probably a Gentile, did not fear God and therefore considered himself under no mandate to be a defender of the defenseless.[31]

The widow came to the judge asking him to secure her rights. The judge refused to act on her behalf. But the woman persisted in her demands for justice; she "kept coming to him" (v. 3). Finally, the judge succumbed to her persistence and said to himself:

> Though I neither fear God nor regard man, yet because this widow bothers me, I will vindicate her, or she will wear me out by her continual coming (v. 5).

The translation that she will "wear him out" may be an understatement. The word he uses could be translated to mean that he fears he will be beaten black and blue! He fears more than mild annoyance. So he grants out of motives of fear and impatience what was hers as a right.

Then Jesus underlines that this judge, unrighteous as he was, granted the woman's request. And he proceeds to put the question to the hearer: "And will not God vindicate his elect, who cry to him day and night" (v. 7)? Here, as in the previous parable, Jesus is not holding up the conduct of an unjust judge for commendation. He is saying that if even an unrighteous judge will grant justice out of fear and self-interest, will not God who is the champion of the poor and the oppressed grant them the justice that they pray for and seek day and night? This ought to move us to confidence in praying.

Thus we glimpse God's Reign when we see one who is powerless persisting until she receives justice. The Reign of God is vindication of the oppressed. It is glimpsed when the oppressed get justice, even when they have to take it from an unwilling and an unjust judge.

And then Jesus adds the question: "Nevertheless, when the Son of Man comes, will he find faith on earth" (v. 8)? This question, viewed as a later addition by some, is at least harmonious with the parable. Once more it puts the question upon those who hear him. If faith is one's disposition to act upon trust in God as the vindicator of the oppressed, is there such a disposition and trust among those who hear the parable? Will there be a body of men and women who have rested their faith in this God of justice and are ready to greet God's Reign?

This parable, as most other parables, has the capacity to cleave us and interrogate us to the depths. If having faith entails looking to God as the One who vindicates the powerless, the parable scrutinizes the reader to see if that faith is to be found in him or her. Does the reader not only believe in but rely upon the vindication of God? Does this vindication for the powerless matter when compared to the vindication offered by *this* age and this world (*aion*), such as money, reputation, position, and all the conventional credentials by which we seek to vindicate ourselves? We see a glimpse of God's Reign when we see one who is powerless demand and obtain for herself the justice that is hers. Can we rejoice at the vision of one who is without power securing for herself what is rightfully hers, or is this a threat? "Nevertheless, when the Son of Man comes, will he find faith on earth" (Luke 18:8)?

JUDGMENT BEGINNING EVEN NOW

In any study of Jesus' teachings, people inevitably face the question: How did Jesus understand God's Reign? Was the

Reign of God something that was already happening in his ministry, or was he simply announcing something that was coming soon? These questions have long occupied students of the New Testament.[32] That Jesus understood God's Reign both as present and yet as still to come has been the assumption throughout this discussion of the parables. He spoke of God's Reign being "at hand" and referred to the signs that Satan's forces were overthrown. Yet the full manifestation of God's Reign was still in the future, an event to be anticipated with confidence and hope.

The view that in Christ God's Reign has appeared and is still to come in its fullness is confirmed in part by Jesus' teaching on the judgment. Jesus taught both that the judgment of God's Reign is in process and that the final judgment will be manifest at some point in the future. Two parables are cited here both as statements of Jesus' teaching on judgment and as instances in which believers are encouraged to be assured of God's Reign. In the face of those who believe that God's Reign tarries unduly, these parables teach that judgment is already taking place.

The Parable of the Closed Door
(Luke 13:24-30)

According to the Parable of the Closed Door, the door to God's Reign is still open. Yet the listener should not assume that the invitation so freely extended to all is an indefinite one. At a certain time, says the parable, the householder will close and lock the door. Then, when it is too late, many will seek his attention trying to get in. And at that time the householder will no longer admit them. They will appeal to their casual ties with the lord of the house: "We ate and drank in your presence, and you taught in our streets" (Luke 13:26). But the answer to the lord of the household is definite: "I tell you, I do not know where you come from; depart from me, all you workers of iniquity" (Luke 13:27).

The vision of judgment functions both as assurance and as warning. It is a projection into the future of the judgment that is beginning even now. Those who think that, through casual acquaintance with Jesus or through their heritage as sons and daughters of Abraham, they have special privilege are to be sadly disillusioned.

This parable both assured that the judgment of God's Reign

would come and warned those who would feel the force of that judgment. No one, therefore, should feel assured of her or his standing merely because of membership in a certain community or even because of casual association with Jesus (Luke 13:26). Assurance was promised for those who entered wholeheartedly into God's Reign while the door was yet open. And it concludes with the familiar assurance and warning: "And behold, some are last who will be first, and some are first who will be last" (Luke 13:30). And the reader is to determine for herself or himself whether this word is assuring or threatening.

The Parable of the Last Judgment
(Matt. 25:31-46)

There is some question whether the Parable of the Last Judgment can properly be called a parable. The comparison cast between the judgment of God's Reign and the separation of sheep from the goats contains many parabolic elements. Yet at the same time, it, like a few other parables that we have studied, contains significant elements of allegory and of prophetic visions.

In its literary form, it bears significant resemblances to other visions of the last judgment. In Ezekiel, we hear God saying: "As for you, my flock, thus says the Lord God: Behold, I judge between sheep and sheep, rams and he-goats" (34:17). In the Similitudes of Enoch (from the period of 94–79 B.C.), there is a vivid picture of the separation of the righteous from the unrighteous before the Throne of the Messiah.[33] Other similar visions appear in the Ezra Apocalypse that is dated approximately A.D. 100.[34] In Matthew's Gospel, the parable is an elaboration of Matthew 16:27 (Mark 8:38/Luke 9:26). In both of those passages, the Son of Man is pictured as the coming Judge. The picture given is intimately bound up with Jewish apocalyptic thought prevailing during the time of Jesus. But the force of the parable or vision bears the unmistakable mark of Jesus' own teaching.

It is not a simple matter to single out the various participants in the drama of the last judgment. They appear as follows: (1) The Son of Man, with all his angels (v. 31); (2) the "nations" (which means the Gentiles in Matthew's usage), both those who have joined God's Reign and those who have not; (3) the king (v. 34); and; (4) the "brethren" (v. 40).

The "Father" refers to God, but God is not pictured as Judge in this parable. The Judge is the king, or the Son of Man. While Jesus does not identify himself as Son of Man or king explicitly (and Jesus nowhere else designates himself as king),[35] the clear implication from Matthew's account is that Christ is Judge.

The king is pictured as sitting on the throne. Before the Judge stand all the nations, meaning the Gentiles. The sheep are separated from the goats, as it was customary to do in the mixed flocks of the Palestinian shepherds. In the evening the shepherd separated them so that the goats who were harmed by the cold could be led into shelter and the sheep who liked the open air could be bedded down outside.[36] The sheep are of more value than the goats and thus inherit the favored position on the right.

Technically the scene that is before us is not a trial but a sentencing. The judgment that informs the sentencing has been going on all along. The Gentiles are before the Judge. The Jews are either those who have joined God's Reign and have responded to Christ among the "brethren," or they are among those who have not heeded God's Reign and therefore are classed with the Gentiles.

With this scene in mind, the only surprise — and hence the source of great assurance — is that the judgment has been taking place all along. Those who were being tried didn't even know that it was going on! Here are "heathen" welcomed into the inheritance of God who were utterly astounded that they had been dealing with the Lord daily. And the same surprise was in store for those who thought themselves righteous. In their response or lack of a response to the most wretched of people — the hungry, the thirsty, the stranger, the naked, the sick, and the imprisoned — they were face-to-face with the Lord. So the evidence was in before anyone knew the trial was taking place! For in responding to those who were disclosed to be Christ's brothers and sisters, they were reckoning with the things of God's Reign.

Whether one understands this as promise or threat, of course, depends upon where one stands with regard to God's Reign. Those who already understood God's Reign in this light have reason for great joy. Those who have left Christ unheeded in the form of the "wretched of the earth" find this parable a hard saying.

But what of the "brethren" who are embraced by Jesus? Where are they in this parable? They are by Jesus' own declaration in solidarity with him and he with them. As a body, they participate in the judgment and sentencing, with the Son of Man as their representative.[37] Those who have left the needy unheeded or who have shared in creating their need now know that their *victim* has become their *judge*. And those who have seen Christ in the needy now find the one whom they have helped to be their *advocate*. Consistent with the parables throughout, God's Reign promises a dramatic reversal.

The Parable of the Talents
(Matt. 25:14–30 / Luke 19:12–27)

A further indication of the judgment that is taking place even now is in a pair of parables that have the same structure, though different details. The two parables probably came originally from the same tradition but Luke's version has become mingled with a popular rabbinic theme of a nobleman leaving to receive authority over a kingdom and then returning with kingly authority. Matthew's account concerns simply "a man" who was going on a journey and entrusted his servants with five, two, and one talents respectively.[38]

The emphasis, when the master returned, was on the servant's productivity. Since they were slaves, all that they gained belonged to their master. The first two who had received five and two talents had multiplied the amount through skillful investment, doubling its worth. The center of attention, however, is upon the third. Excusing himself by reference to his master's reputation for hardness and retribution, the third servant said that he had merely held on to what he was given and now had it to return to him. The first two servants were rewarded by being entrusted with greater responsibility. The third had the one talent given to him taken away and given instead to the one who had ten talents.

The details of Luke's account differ considerably. Here the nobleman goes away to receive authority. On his return the productive servants are rewarded with greater political authority. Luke's version also blends in a second plot. Some of the citizens do not wish to be under the authority of the nobleman who is to be appointed to rule over them. They therefore send a delegation. After the empowered nobleman has settled accounts with his servants, he turns to his unwilling subjects and orders that they be slain before him (Luke 19:27). (This addition may refer to an actual historical situation in 4 B.C. in which Archelaus traveled to Rome to be confirmed in his rule over Judaea. A group of fifty Jews journeyed to Rome to protest his appointment. He was nonetheless appointed, and, when he returned, he exacted retribution that was not quickly forgotten.)[39]

Jesus likely first used this parable against the religious officials who were entrusted with the Word of God. Their zeal to protect the religious tradition from any contact with the heathen and to purify the nation itself from all alien influence is suggested by the servant who held tenaciously to the money rather than putting it to productive use.

For those Christians following Christ's resurrection, however, this parable naturally would have suggested their own situation. They had been entrusted with the Gospel, and the Lord would soon be returning and would settle accounts with them on the manner in which they had exercised their stewardship. Judgment was already taking place.

The Parables of the Barren Fig Tree and the Net
(Luke 13:6–9; Matt. 13:47–50)

The theme of judgment was suggested earlier in this chapter when we examined the Parable of the Weeds. In that parable we are encouraged to allow the weeds to remain for the time being with the wheat confident that, at harvest time, the two will be separated and the weeds cast into the fire.

Two other parables illustrate this same general theme. In the Parable of the Net, there is reference to the gathering together not merely of the good and the bad but of all varieties of people. Persons of a variety of aptitudes, backgrounds, moral attainment and religious standing have responded to the call to God's Reign. The figure used is that of a large net that is drawn between two boats or pulled by one boat with long lines to the shore.[40] As the net is pulled to the shore, all the varieties of sea life are gathered together. When the net is drawn ashore, then the process of separation begins. All fish without scales and fins are discarded as unclean according to the Law (see Leviticus 11:10–12). Those that can be eaten are gathered for sale.

The effect of the parable is to provide assurance that the judgment of the Reign of God will surely take place. At the same time, it proclaims that there is still time for repentance and turning toward God's Reign.

A similar message is suggested by the Parable of the Fig Tree. Luke's introduction to the parable relates two incidents of sudden and appalling suffering that were inflicted upon people. One concerned Jews from Galilee who were struck down by Pilate while they were offering their sacrifices in the Temple in Jerusalem (Luke 13:1). In a second incident, eighteen persons were killed when a tower, a part of the fortifications of Jerusalem, collapsed and fell upon them (13:4). In both these instances, Jesus separates himself from the notion that those who were thus stricken were being punished for sins more extreme than others who lived in Jerusalem at that time. And he points to these examples of sudden destruction as reason for his hearers carefully to consider the call into God's Reign and to repent before the final judgment is visited upon them.

In the parable, Jesus tells of a man who had a fig tree planted in a garden, likely a plot that included grapevines and a variety of fruit trees. For three years, he looked on the fig tree to find some fruit, and there was none. There was no reason, thought the man, to allow this tree to continue to take up space and to draw nutrients from the soil while bearing no fruit. So he commanded his gardener to cut it down. The gardener intervened on behalf of the tree and suggested that with fertilizer and loosening the soil around the roots it might produce in another year. After one more year without productivity, then it might be cut down. Once again this parable assures the listener that the judgment that is implicit in God's Reign is beginning and will be consummated in the future. Yet there is still time for turning toward God's Reign.

The Parable of the Wicked Tenants
(Mark 12:1–12 / Matt. 21:33–44 / Luke 20:9–18)

This parable, although sometimes interpreted as conveying a different message, can be included legitimately among those sayings of Jesus that offer assurance of the coming of God's Reign. The story is really an allegory, a form that Jesus usually did not employ.

The owner of the vineyard, as the context of the story makes evident, is one who lives outside the country. He may be a foreigner. Large regions of Galilee were formed into estates that were owned by foreign landlords. Resentment and rebellion against foreign ownership, natural enough in any situation, were especially near the surface in Jesus' day.[41]

In most lease agreements, the owner was entitled to a portion of the crop in exchange for the use of the land. It is this legitimate share that he sent his servant to collect (Mark 12:2/ Matt. 21:34/Luke 20:10). When the tenants have wounded, humiliated, and killed several servants, the owner sends his son, reasoning perhaps that they would not dare bring harm to such a one in authority and that the son could at last put down the uprising of the tenants.

But the tenants had other ideas. Seeing the son, they may have assumed that the father, the owner, was dead. They reasoned that, if they seized and killed the heir, the inheritance, now his, would becomes theirs (Mark 12:7 and parallels). There was legal provision in Jesus' time that, in some circumstances, an inheritance would be declared ownerless property and might be claimed by anyone, with preference going to the one who claimed it first.[42] Possibly such a law was in the background of the tenants' thinking. Otherwise, their supposition about claiming the property for themselves by killing the heir would make little sense. So the son also was killed, and his body was thrown over the wall of the vineyard, an added insult.

Then Jesus put the question: "What will the owner of the vineyard do?" (Mark 12:9a). Even if Jesus did not answer his own question the answer would be quite clear. The owner's legitimate return had been denied him; his servants were wounded or slain; and his own son was killed and humiliated. The least he would do would be to put out the tenants and put his vineyard in new hands. And this Jesus' hearers would assume could be done quite handily, for there are cases on record in which landowners similarly affronted called on the occupation government for assistance and collected the debt with the help of an imported force of cavalry.[43]

All three Gospel writers report that the religious establishment understood that the parable was aimed at them (Matt. 21:45/Mark 12:12/Luke 20:19). And well they might! The parable is one of judgment and is quite consistent with the message of Jesus' other parables. The religious leaders, having been given stewardship of the Word of God, had not recognized the fulfillment of the Reign of God when it came into their midst. They had not borne the fruit they were charged to bear. Therefore, God's Reign was not to be in their hands. It would be turned over to others.

And who were the others? If we are to heed the other parables told by Jesus, the ones who will receive God's Reign are those who even then were responding to it — the poor and disinherited, the outcast — those, in short, who had so little to expect from this age that they cast their full reliance upon God's Reign. The parable is at once a warning and a source of assurance in the judgment that is to come and the gift of God's Reign to those who are prepared to receive it.

Now the story is so strikingly parallel to Israel's history that it was inevitable that allegorical details would be added in the process of interpreting its significance for the early Christians. Mark and Matthew quote almost directly from Isaiah 5:1–5 in their preface. This would clarify beyond any doubt to the reader that the vineyard is the nation of Israel, and that God is the rightful owner, as the song from Isaiah clearly states. Mark and Luke refer not only to "his son," as Matthew does, but to a "beloved son" (Mark 12:6/Luke 20:13). This term, used in the instances of only children and hence meaning "only beloved son," is the same term used by all three evangelists to refer to Jesus by a heavenly voice in their accounts of the Baptism and Transfiguration of Jesus (Cf. Matt. 3:17; 17:5; Mark 1:11; 9:7; Luke 3:22; and, in a variant reading, Luke 9:35). Thus the reference to Christ is made even more explicit. Whereas, in Mark, the son is first killed and his body then thrown out of the vineyard (12:8), Matthew and Luke reverse the order (Matt. 21:39 and

Luke 20:15) to make it reflect more clearly the circumstances in which Jesus was crucified outside the city.

These references, plus, no doubt, the quotation from Psalm 118 and the summary of the priests' reaction (Mark 12:12/Matt. 21:45f./Luke 20:18), found their way into the basic story as a way of interpreting its Christological significance. But these additions should not cause us to disregard the central message of the story as Jesus told it. Set as it is by all three evangelists in the portion of Jesus' ministry immediately before his passion, it provides an assuring glimpse of a future when that which is God's is taken away from those who have wounded and slain God's messengers and is put into the stewardship of those who are prepared to enter the era of God's rule.

QUESTIONS AND SUGGESTED METHODS

1. The parables were teaching devices used by Jesus that could be understood by everyone. One did not have to know an "inside" code language in order to experience the truth of what Jesus was saying. To what extent is our proclamation of Christ and God's Reign comprehensible to those outside our churches? What means has the church identified to communicate with those who are not familiar with the religious language used by the church? What cues to do the parables provide for the church?

2. Persons in the group can be asked to identify films or short stories that are comparable to the parables in their effects upon the listener or viewer. These films or short stories might be shared as a part of the group session. One film used extensively by groups, for example, is *The Parable.** Such a film could be viewed and then discussed among group members. What marks do they have in common with the New Testament parables we are studying? How do they assist the viewer to experience the reality to which they refer?

3. Using figures out of your own experience, write a parable of assurance in God's Reign. What images are comparable to the miracle of seed? The parable could be written as a script for

---

The Parable is available in film or video from Ecufilm, 810 12th Ave. South, Nashville, TN 37203 (800-251-4091). Rental fee for film or video is $20.00.

a drama or a motion picture. It might also be phrased into the words for a ballad or folk song.

4. Compose a hymn, litany, or prayer using figures from one or more of the parables studied for this session. That hymn or prayer could be used as a part of the study session.

5. Invite someone who is a bread baker to demonstrate the effect of yeast and leaven before the class, allowing the class to feel the texture of the dough as the kneading and yeast bring about expansion and the bread takes on life.

6. We comprehend the parables best when we are able to interpret them to others. The group may want to provide opportunities in which the parables can be shared. Some may wish to use non-verbal means of sharing the parables. The group should experiment with the communication of the parables by role playing, interpretive dance, or other media.

7. The Parable of the Last Judgment, while picturing the final tribunal, suggests that judgment is a constant process and is intimately related to our relationships with others, particularly the disinherited. What effect does it have upon the stewardship of our common life if we think of judgment as such an ongoing process?

8. As the group nears the end of the study, it would be well to summarize its experiences of the parables. One person could assist by summarizing the list of the characters from the parables compiled in one of the early sessions. What characters now are most vivid in the minds of people of the group? What new discoveries do they associate with these characters? What new insights or questions have the parables prompted in this study? On what themes in Christian faith has there been the most growth during the study?

9. The parables, among other things, are invitations to God's Reign. What barriers, if any, do you feel against your embracing God's Reign? What points of hesitation do you discover in yourself? What forces do you feel prompting you to believe in God's Reign? Do you find similar forces in evidence among Jesus' first hearers? What guidance does their response provide you?

Notes

1. Eta Linnemann, *Jesus of the Parables*, trans. John Sturdy (New York: Harper & Row, 1964), pp. 115f. See also Robert Stein, *An Introduction to the Parables of Jesus* (Philadelphia: Westminster Press, 1981), pp. 36–37.

2. A translation of Mark 4:9 suggested by Ezra P. Gould, *A Critical and Exegetical Commentary on the Gospel According to St. Mark* (New York: Charles Scribner's Sons, 1905), p. 71.

3. T. W. Manson, *The Teaching of Jesus: Studies of Its Form and Content* (Cambridge: Cambridge University Press, 1955 [1931], p. 78.

4. Ibid. See a similar discussion in Joachim Jeremias, *The Parables of Jesus* (New York: Charles Scribner's Sons, 1972), p. 17.

5. See a summary of these conclusions in ibid., pp. 77–79. For a defense of the view that the quote from Isaiah in Matt. 13:14–15 is an interpolation from a later editor, see Jack Dean Kingsbury, *The Parables of Jesus in Matthew 13: A Study in Redaction-Criticism* (Richmond: John Knox Press, 1969), pp. 38–39.

6. See Madeleine Boucher's discussion of these varied types of literature in *The Mysterious Parable: A Literary Study* (Washington: Catholic Biblical Association of America, 1977), pp. 86–89.

7. Ibid., p. 13.

8. Jeremias, *The Parables of Jesus*, pp. 16, 17.

9. See this emphasis in Boucher, *The Mysterious Parable*, p. 24.

10. Ibid., pp. 81ff.

11. The distinction between parables and allegories has been an enduring aspect of the study of the parables, especially after the watershed writing of Adolf Julicher in 1888 (*Die Gleichnisreden Jesu* [Darmstadt: Wissenschaftliche Buchgesellschaft, 1976 (1888, 1889)]). The definitions in the preceding paragraph drew the contrasts between the two as sharply as possible in order to show how parables and allegories, as ideal types, actually differ. Many recent commentators, while building on Julicher's work, nonetheless insist that we should not rule out all aspects of allegory in the parables. Indeed, Boucher holds that allegory and parable logically cannot be divided. "Any parable," she says, "which has both a literal and a metaphorical meaning is an allegory" (*The Mysterious Parable*, p. 21). Perhaps the boldest challenge to the position on allegories formed by Julicher and later writers such as Jeremias and Dodd is that of John Drury (*The Parables in the Gospels: History and Allegory* [London: SPCK, 1985]). He consistently finds allegory in most of the parables of the Gospels and contends that allegory is the norm for the parables and not an exception (p. 155).

12. For illustrations of such allegorical interpretations through Christian history, see Archibald Hunter, *Interpreting the Parables* (Philadel-

phia: Westminster, 1960), pp. 21–41. For a contemporary form of allegorical interpretation, see John Sanford, *The Kingdom Within* (Philadelphia: J. B. Lippincott, 1970). A helpful history of the interpretation of the parables is given in Warren S. Kissinger, *The Parables of Jesus: A History of Interpretation and Bibliography* (Metuchen, N.J.: Scarecrow Press, 1979), pp. 1–230.

13. Manson, *The Sayings of Jesus*, pp. 193f.

14. Jeremias, *Parables of Jesus*, p. 224.

15. W. O. E. Oesterley, *The Gospel Parables* (London: Society for Promoting Christian Knowledge, 1936), p. 61.

16. Ibid., pp. 60–61.

17. Manson, *The Sayings of Jesus*, p. 123.

18. Oesterley, *The Gospel Parables*, p. 77.

19. Manson, *The Sayings of Jesus*, p. 123.

20. Sherman E. Johnson, "Exegesis on the Gospel According to St. Matthew," *The Interpreter's Bible*, vol. 7, George A. Buttrick, ed. (New York: Abingdon-Cokesbury, 1951), p. 417.

21. This account draws upon background provided in Kenneth Ewing Bailey, *Poet and Peasant: A Literary Cultural Approach to the Parables in Luke* (Grand Rapids, Mich.: William B. Eerdmans, 1976), pp. 122ff.

22. Ibid., p. 123, n. 23.

23. Ibid., p. 122.

24. J. Duncan M. Derrett, *Studies in the New Testament*, vol. 3: *Midrash, Haggadah, and the Character of the Community* (Leiden: E. J. Brill, 1982), p. 34.

25. Norman Perrin, *Rediscovering the Teaching of Jesus* (New York: Harper & Row, 1976), p. 128.

26. Bailey, *Poet and Peasant*, p. 133.

27. Ibid., pp. 130–133.

28. Indeed, "persistence" is the word Fitzmyer uses in his translation of Luke 11:8 (*The Gospel According to Luke, x–xxiv*, p. 909). The Jerusalem Bible has also used "persistence" in v. 8.

29. See Derrett, *Midrash, Haggadah, and the Character of the Community*, p. 37ff.

30. G. B. Caird, *The Gospel of St. Luke* (Baltimore: Penguin Books, 1963), p. 201. See for example: Exodus 22:22; Deuteronomy 10:18; Psalms 68:5; Isaiah 1:17; Jeremiah 22:3.

31. The portrait of the unjust judge is a negative example of the upright judge in Ecclesiasticus, or the Wisdom of Jesus the Son of Sirach, 35:13–18 (from the *Apocrypha*, Revised Standard Version [New York: Thomas Nelson & Sons, 1957]). This connection is made by John Drury, *The Parables in the Gospels*, p. 153.

32. For an overview of these discussions, see Norman Perrin, *The Kingdom of God in the Teaching of Jesus* (London: SCM, 1963).

33. Enoch 62 and 63. Quoted in Oesterley, *The Gospel Parables*, p. 152.

34. Quoted in ibid., p. 152.

35. Jeremias, *Parables of Jesus*, p. 206.

36. Ibid.

37. Manson, *The Sayings of Jesus*, pp. 217 and 249–250. Not all interpreters of the parables will identify "the brethren" with the poor and needy *in general*. John Donahue holds that in Matthew's perspective "the brethren" are to be understood as Christian disciples or missionaries (*The Gospel in Parable* [Philadelphia: Fortress Press, 1988], pp. 120ff.). He sees this identification, however, not as a sectarian position but as an acknowledgment of their role in the justification of the whole world in God's Reign and the manner in which "the world will be made 'right' or 'just' when the way the least are treated becomes the norm of action" (p. 124). A similar identification of "the brethren" is suggested by Stein (*An Introduction to the Parables of Jesus* [Philadelphia: Westminster Press, 1981], p. 138).

38. "Talents" in this case was only a unit of money (worth about one thousand dollars). Our use of this word to refer to aptitudes and skills stems from this parable, but in the Greek the word referred only to a sum of money (designating a weight of silver or gold).

39. Jeremias, *Parables of Jesus*, p. 59.

40. Ibid., p. 225.

41. Extensive evidence attesting to the historical conditions in Palestine reflected in this story is cited in Klyne Snodgrass, *The Parable of the Wicked Tenants* (Tübingen: J. C. B. Mohr, 1983), see pp. 35, 37, and 40. Drury believes the parable is strictly allegorical and does not reflect a realistic historical situation (*The Parables in the Gospels*, p. 66).

42. Ibid., pp. 75–76.

43. C. H. Dodd, *Parables of the Kingdom* (London: Nisbet & Co., 1935), p. 127.

Part III

Living in God's Reign

Chapter 8

Living in God's Reign

We have attempted to examine the meaning of the parables in the context of Jesus' ministry. But the question that concerns us most, of course, is the hearing of the parables upon our present and our future. What message do they bear for us today? How do they illuminate the choices we face and the possibilities before us?

Throughout the study we have noticed the ability of the parables to interpret their hearers. Those who brought charges against Jesus found that they themselves were searched out and examined by the parables.

Likely this has been our experience as well. A part of us has rejoiced at the return of the prodigal, but another part of us may have been frightened and afraid at the prospect of allowing such an offender back into the family without "learning his lesson." One side of our nature may have found it possible to rejoice when those who arrived late in the day were given a whole day's wage, but the other side likely felt resentment for lack of "fair treatment." The parables cleave us to the core.

In this chapter we shall focus upon this capacity of the parables to help us to understand ourselves and our world. And we shall examine how as an expression of our responsibility for this age we may glimpse and give our loyalty to the age that is to come.

THE WORLD OF THE PARABLES AND OUR OWN

A first step in allowing the parables to interpret us is in recognizing the important parallels between our world and the world of the parables. In spite of impressive differences between Jesus' time and our own, there are central questions and concerns that are common to both.

The End of an Age

Jesus' contemporaries were convinced that the age in which they lived was coming to an end. Many despaired so thoroughly about the structures of their age that they looked forward to its complete overthrow and the consequent institution of the Reign of God. The prayer prayed through the centuries, "Come, Lord Jesus," was a plea to end this present world and to initiate God's Reign.

In our society today we hear voices saying that the present "age" or "world" of consumption and the despoilment of nature must end if humankind is to survive. Such persons speak of the need for a basic transformation, though their entreaties are most often cast in secular terms that sound far removed from the imagery of the Bible.

In some instances, persons who voice these concerns do little more than express their forebodings of despair. Some years ago Robert Heilbroner, for example, surveyed the massive problems that confront this planet — the exhaustion of raw materials, the potential outbreak of wars between the developed and the poverty-ridden nations, the use of weapons of massive destruction, or sustained and widespread starvation — and came to a melancholy judgment about the immediate future: "If then by the question 'Is there hope for man?' we ask whether it is possible to meet the challenges of the future without the payment of a fearful price, the answer must be: No, there is no such hope."[1]

The outlook for the future voiced by Heilbroner is similar in many important ways to the expectations of many to whom Jesus spoke, but without their hope. Like many in the time of Jesus, Heilbroner believes that the time of crisis is rapidly approaching. All of us — whether we are conscious of the coming crisis or oblivious of its approach — will undergo suffering and travail (repression, starvation, environmental pollution, and other such perils arising out of our profligate past). And only after that period of suffering and adjustment is past, after "the dangerous mentality of industrial civilization itself" is abandoned,[2] can there be a more favorable prospect for the human race.

Despite the secular terms in which these conclusions are expressed, the major outlines parallel those of Jewish apocalypticism. The apocalyptic writers also envisioned the swift coming of a crisis in which both the faithful and the unfaithful would suffer the woes of the ending of an age. Then, when the wickedness of that age was completely consumed, the faithful could look with expectation to the creation of a new heaven and a new earth. The apocalyptic writers foresaw no painless escape from the impending suffering. Yet, because they believed God to be at work in the affairs of history, they looked to the future with hope.

But it is not merely those who see and despair who voice for us the prospect of the end of an age. There are those who believe that difficult and massive changes will be required of us but that, with the right choices, the human race can avoid catastrophe.

Willis Harman, an engineer and futurist, has written for several years on the theme that humankind must undergo a fundamental transformation or perish. The dilemmas that confront us, says Harman, are not capable of solution within a paradigm or model of the world built upon the notion of growth, acquisition, accelerated consumption, and use of fossil fuels to replace animal energy.

It is possible for the human race to decide to survive, Harman contends. But, if we are to do so, we must as a human race undergo a profound change in our assumptions and values. It is a change so profound, he continues, that we should label it by the Greek word *metanoia*, meaning "a fundamental transformation of mind."[3] Remarkably, *metanoia* was the same root word that Jesus used to call people to God's Reign: "The time is fulfilled, and the kingdom of God is at hand; repent [*metanoeite*], and believe in the gospel" (Mark 1:15).

The nature of the impending transformation is outlined in some detail in the best-selling volume by Marilyn Ferguson entitled *The Aquarian Conspiracy: Personal and Social Transforma-*

tion in the 1980s.[4] In this book, the author declares that we are living in a time of fulfillment of hopes and dreams long held by the people. She quotes approvingly that this is an era in which "apocalyptic visions are to be fulfilled" and that "we are on the brink of a new life, entering a new domain."[5]

Discernment of this new reality, she continues, depends on a deeper way of seeing. One cannot be persuaded that the new reality is here; the hidden significance of this new reality must be perceived by a new way of knowing, by new eyes.[6] It is insight in a new dimension.[7] Since this new dimension cannot be argued for as a conventional reality, the author presents it in examples, metaphors, and analogies. And once those figures of speech have been appropriated, they reveal a whole new order, a new world, that makes everything intelligible.[8]

Further, Ferguson contends that this new reality has formed a new community that she terms a "conspiracy." In terms that remind the student of the New Testament of the formation of the church in Acts by the breathing in of the Holy Spirit, she explains that "conspiracy" is an appropriate term, meaning literally "to breathe together."[9]

She lauds the visionaries of the new reality as ones who have persisted. "They have chosen life, whatever the cost."[10] She promises that those who join this "conspiracy" will find that it helps the individual make sense of the totality of his or her life, family relationships, community relationships, and view of the world. It also helps a person to understand his or her place in history. For some, she concedes, such a conspiracy might seem a last gasp before ecological, totalitarian, or nuclear tragedy. Yet she paraphrases the thoughts of one of the new order of visionaries with this promise:

> We stand on the brink of a new age..., the age of an open world, a time of renewal when a fresh release of spiritual energy in the world culture may unleash new possibilities. "The sum of all our days is just our beginning."
>
> Seen with new eyes, our lives can be transformed from accidents into adventures.... After our tragic wars, alienation, and the bruising of the planet, perhaps this is the answer Wallace Stevens meant — after the final No, the Yes on which the future of the world depends.[11]

All these promising possibilities, despite their significance
for the whole world, come by way of individuals. This is not,
we are assured, because of an innate trust in human nature but
by "trust in the transformative process itself."[12] This process is
not identified with God, though it comes through the pages of
the book to function as deity since it is the object of trust and
commitment.[13]

However one agrees or disagrees with the contents of *The
Aquarian Conspiracy*, it is clear that the assumptions and outlines of its proposed "new age" are quite different from the Reign
of God proclaimed and embodied by Jesus. It is equally apparent, however, that the widespread interest in this book and the
extensive network of people who share its views indicate a large
number of people who sense they are ending one age and entering another. To whatever extent people of today share the
intuition that one epoch is ending, they are well prepared to put
themselves in the place of those who first heard Jesus teach in
parables.

Focus upon the Future

Whenever people sense that they live in precarious times, the
question of the future is raised with new urgency and concern.
We have already discussed the forms that that focus took among
the Jewish people at the time of Jesus. In the centuries that have
followed, the advent of serious threats has been the occasion for
new understandings of God's purposes and for the reality of the
divine promise for the future. Hope has often flourished when
the immediate times were most desperate. *ukraine*

There is much to suggest that uncertainties of the immediate time have raised the question of the future for us with more
intensity than in previous generations. In the past few decades,
scores of corporations and institutes for the future have been
formed throughout the world. Books and popular magazines
describe for us the world of the future that awaits us. Environ-
mentalists and energy experts are consulted with the seriousness
and urgency that once attended visits to the oracles.

Concern for the future is the most obvious context in which
people of today — secular as we may seem — raise questions
that are essentially religious in nature. Religious faith, among

other things, concerns itself with those elements in our individual and collective lives that are not at our disposal — with that which inspires awe, dread, or joy. Religious faith refers to the ultimate reality with which we all must reckon. For many twentieth-century Americans, the place where such feelings are encountered most frequently is the future. The time immediately ahead has for us the same urgency that historically has been focused upon considerations of heaven and hell.[14] The network newscast was addressing our condition when it headed the report on the environment with the question, "Can the world be saved?"

To whatever extent we share this focus upon the future, we are a part of the world of the parables. The preoccupation of Jesus' contemporaries with the question of the future has been evident throughout. Just because their present was so precarious, they looked eagerly for some sign for their future. Simeon likely represented many of the righteous and devout at the time of Jesus who steadfastly scanned the future, "looking for the consolation of Israel" (Luke 2:25).

The Search for a Messiah

The focus for the concern about the future among people in Jesus' time was the heavenly Son of Man who would descend to redeem the fallen human condition. They hoped for the "anointed one" or "Christ" who would act on God's behalf to lead the people out of their servile state. The question that John's disciples put to Jesus likely was on the lips of many as they looked expectantly for the Lord's Messiah: "Are you he who is to come, or shall we look for another?" (Luke 7:19).

A version of the quest for a Messiah runs through our culture as well. At the level of our popular diversions and entertainment, there is enduring fascination with the theme of the figure who comes from without to redeem a situation. What are our western novels and films if not salvation stories with the saving figure (the heroic lawman) from outside who redeems life in the frontier town? The Superman story, created in the midst of the Depression of the 1930s, is a recurring theme in popular entertainment. There is little that is subtle about the messianic character of Superman's mission.[15] He is transported to earth as an infant from his home on Krypton. Though just an infant, he bears with him the wisdom of other spheres. He possesses gifts to work wonders for the sake of humans in need. Nor should we overlook the saving mission of Mary Poppins, who floats down from the heavens with an umbrella. When she has made things right for the Banks household, she is assumed again into the skies.[16] However superficial the messianic stories of popular entertainment may be, the persistence with which they recur indicates at least that there is a receptiveness toward and a fascination with messianic themes.

On a somewhat more serious level, we have a yearning for figures of messianic proportion in our political life. When we grow skeptical and cynical about the capacities of government, we often seek some figure from outside the government to set it right again. We seem virtually unwilling to consider a candidate unless that person promises to work wonders beyond the capacity of any human to accomplish. Just as the medieval artists painted halos around the saintly to evidence the aura of holiness, we bathe our political leaders in the glow of the television screen and communicate something very much like a holy or superhuman aura about them as well.

Our yearning for salvation through messianic powers is often fixed upon the sciences and the techniques to which they give rise. Robert Coles, the Harvard psychologist, has said that our search for salvation through the social sciences has populated affluent suburban sections of our communities with "crypto-churches." They are presided over, says Coles, by the family counselors, sex counselors, and group therapists who serve as their priests.[17]

But perhaps the most obvious form that our quest for the secular messiah takes is in our hopes for the products of laboratory research. In our common conversation we frequently reveal the hope and confident expectation that laboratory research will find a cure for cancer, or develop superconductors, or discover a means for feeding the hungry of the world. Many persons who would disassociate themselves from messianic faith altogether nonetheless figuratively search the faces of scientists in the research centers to ask if this is the one who is to come or if they should look for another.

None of this is to deny that God does often work wonder through the disciplined commitment of persons in the sciences as in other human pursuits. It is to suggest, however, that in some of our expectations associated with the sciences, we show hopes of a messianic and possibly of an idolatrous nature. It is to suggest as well that in our quests for some one or some group to deliver us from our distress we share a concern that was prominent in the imaginations of those who were first encountered by Jesus. To the degree that we share their concern we also share important qualities of their world.

PARABLES AS ALTERNATIVE FUTURES

The Shock of the Unexpected

The principal impact of the parables was to disclose an alternative view of what was at work in the happenings of daily life. For those who thought that life was thoroughly predictable, for those who thought that the Age to Come could be summoned by scrupulous adherence to the Law, the parables represented a severe jolt.

The parables portray the intrusion of novelty and grace into events that otherwise were proceeding to quite a different conclusion. Under no stretch of conventional reckoning could one imagine the miserable Lazarus being regaled at the table of Abraham or could one fancy the hovel of a poor widow as the scene for the outbreak of joy and celebration. But just when people thought that they had their world under control, just when they felt that they could assure a favorable standing for themselves in the order of things, the parables jolted them off balance by offering an alternative view.

It is not inappropriate, therefore, to suggest that the most natural response to many — if not most — of the parables is surprise. They portray a series of events that the hearer assumes will issue in a certain consequence. Then suddenly there is a dramatic surprise, a jolting reversal.

In the Parable of the Last Judgment, the blessed and the

condemned both are surprised to learn that judgment has been taking place all along. They are amazed to hear that matters of highest importance have depended upon the fate of those thought to be of least consequence, the poor and the dispossessed. Surprise is perhaps not the word to use here; we might better call it shock! In the Parable of the Marriage Feast, those who were normally invited to such affairs were excluded, and the banquet table was filled with those who were utterly astounded to be invited guests at such an affair! Shock at an unexpected turn of events is an appropriate response.

Deliverance from the Demonic

The parables testify as well to the subjection of the evil spirits in the ministry of Jesus and the advent of the Reign of God. Jesus compared his ministry to the one who entered the strong man's house, bound him, and then plundered his goods (Matt. 12:29/Mark 3:27/Luke 11:21, 22). Now that God's Reign was at hand, those who had been unjustly held in check by the powers of Satan were now released and free. Jesus freed people from those forces that hitherto had visited upon them illness, fear, isolation from others, and many forms of bizarre behavior.

To whatever extent that we today feel trapped by forces and systems not under our control (and it is hard to conceive of any sensitive person today not feeling so constrained), we should be able to understand what the authors of the New Testament meant. Many persons, for example, want to develop friendships or lasting marriages, yet despite their best intent find themselves isolated and alone. In other aspects of our individual lives as well we find something alien intruding to undo our deepest wishes. Sometimes we unconsciously acknowledge this feeling by confessing, "I don't know what has gotten into me."

On the global level, the tragedy is multiplied many-fold. It would be hard to find anyone so morally and spiritually dead as to consent to the starvation of another human being. Yet, in a world that produces enough food to feed everyone, whole portions of the earth's population suffer crippling malnutrition and starvation. What has gone awry to account for such massive, unnecessary suffering? When we struggle with such questions, we are perhaps in a position to understand, in part, what the biblical writers referred to as the evil spirits or the principalities and powers. They believed that these hostile forces were organized into alliances and hierarchies and that they subverted the intent of whole communities of people as well as of individuals.

The message of the parables and of the whole ministry of Jesus is that these forces are identified, addressed, and undone by Jesus, the bearer of God's Reign. While their sting and power are not fully eliminated, the victory has already been won. It is possible to entertain a new future knowing that the powers that distort and corrupt life are not final. As another witness was later to testify:

> He [Jesus] himself likewise partook of the same nature, that through death he might destroy him who has the power of death ... and deliver all those who through fear of death were subject to lifelong bondage. (Heb. 2:14, 15)

It is not our intent to step back into the thought forms of Jesus' day and suggest that we picture demonic powers as individual entities. We simply want to acknowledge that the biblical references to evil spirits identify experiences that we and our contemporaries undergo and with which we must reckon. Whether we speak of evil spirits and powers and principalities or about the global systems (economic, ecological, or political) that have slipped perilously out of human control, the effect on humans is much the same. More importantly, when we speak of Jesus Christ overcoming the evil spirits, we voice our faith that the last word over all the massive systems of this world — and of any other world that is yet to be — is uttered by God. And that word will confirm all that we have come to know in Jesus Christ. Therefore, we are not consumed by fear, or bondage, or despair. Without for a moment denying the fearful barriers that lie between us and a more promising future, we believe that God is struggling to accomplish the divine purposes in this world and that we are bid to join that struggle. The parables set forth an alternative possibility. And, in that, we find reason for hope and for redoubled efforts to give voice to that hope in our midst.

THE GIFT OF A NEW EXPECTATION

In a situation confronted by the challenge that looms before the human race, the most powerful force for hope is an alternative view of the future. Few of us are inspired into new forms of living by dread or fear. We are changed when we are possessed with the vision of a new possibility, one that lures us on until it is achieved or at least approached from afar. We crave a new beginning and a restored vision.

One of the disturbing elements of our situation today is that so few of our visions of the future are capable of attracting our loyalty or sacrifice. "In our time we seem to have finally exhausted the central images of the future that have pulled us, however erratically in the past. These images are not dead, for they still have their adherents. However, none seem to have the power to energize the public imagination in any collective sense.... In short, we have no comforting images of greatness and progress that speak to all of us; we have no common roots in some dominant vision, no shared dream uniquely fitting our historic period."[18] These words written by a futurist reveal a major dimension of our predicament.

We have grown accustomed to thinking of the future as the promise of more consumer goods. It is particularly hard for those who already have much of the world's goods to imagine a future in any terms other than "more of the same." Yet that future offers us little hope. Does the possession of two television sets instead of one make us twice as happy? More importantly, what hope is there for the earth's poor if the future is simply a replay of the past?

The most formidable obstacle for hope is not the presence of staggering challenges in the future. It is that loss of vision that, recognizing the inadequacies of the present, is incapable of imagining a future on any other terms.[19] The Pharisees had thought that the secret of the future could be reduced to predictable patterns. So far as they were concerned, the terms that determined the future were obvious and well in hand. The parables released in the midst of that predictability a new vision, a fresh possibility. Astounding as it was, the parables allowed one to experience the present and the future as the work of God's decisive, gracious action. For those who staked all on this Reign of God, the future was qualitatively new, and they entered into the joy of God's Reign.

Today there is desperate need for visions of the future that promise a state of affairs that is decidedly new and not just a predictable consequence of present assumptions. Basic assumptions about national defense, for example, were formed when it was a commonly accepted assumption that the accumulation of destructive power could protect a nation against outside threat. Now it is general knowledge that there is an equivalent of twenty tons of TNT for every person on the face of the earth. We possess the power to kill every person twelve times! Yet we are less secure than ever.

What we need in our situation is an alternative future, the vision of new possibilities for the future. Yet there is a rigid orthodoxy among planners on both sides of the struggle that can envision no response other than the further accumulation of power. Colossal sums of money and other resources are taken from the hungry and fed into the insatiable appetite of the war machine in this country and other nations throughout the world. So long as the assumptions prevail that led to the arms race in the first place, we are unlikely to find alternative visions that will allow us to break out of the suicidal trend that sweeps us along.

The parables represent a most profound basis for change and for hope, for they depict the reality of God's Reign in which significantly different possibilities are to be found. They provide an alternative future for which to live. Just as the sower, in casting seed into the ground, is living out the vision of the harvest that follows the decaying seed, so the one who today is grasped by the force of God's Reign offers his or her efforts confident that our modest efforts today will yield results far out of proportion to our power and ability. The parables set forth an alternative future by first freeing our spirits to imagine and dream a new expectation.

A TANGIBLE HOPE

The effect of Jesus' ministry was to liberate people from the inevitability that hitherto had held them in its clutches. The power of God's Reign visible in Jesus' ministry was indeed the power of the future that was even then "spilling over" into the present. In the parables, an isolated happening is shown to exhibit marks of God's Reign. Those infused with hope can detect in the otherwise insignificant experience a tangible sign of a new future.

People who came to Jesus to be healed often found themselves challenged to produce a tangible sign. The paralytic who was formerly a passive victim is challenged to stand up by himself (Mark 2:11). The man who had waited thirty-eight years for someone to heal him now hears Jesus tell him to move to the healing pool on his own (John 5:8)! God's Reign made its impact upon the present through provisional signs, anticipatory tokens, and a tangible hope.

We may illustrate the power of a tangible sign in producing a new future by the process of community development. Any organizer in a community of people knows that one of his or her first tasks is to dispel the notion that the situation in that community is inevitable, that there is something preordained that things should be the way they are. "In order for the oppressed to be able to wage the struggle for their liberation, they must perceive the reality of oppression not as a closed world from which there is no exit, but as a limiting situation that they can transform."[20]

The principal task in "consciousness-raising" or community organizing is to help people act in different ways in order that they can begin to envision their community and world in different ways. If a community wants to act together to improve its neighborhood, it is important that it undertake manageable tasks at the first so that it can experience what it is like to accomplish something together. This helps the community to erect an alternative future, purged of the demonic inevitability, the fatalism that may have marked its past. The first undertakings of a newly organized neighborhood are glimpses of the unity and power that they will one day have as a community. They offer tangible signs of hope.

To participate as pioneers in time, to interpret the future through the perspective of the parables, is to have an alternative future that stands as a challenge to the present and a source of hope and struggle for the time to come. Such an alternative future that we have seen in Jesus Christ provides hope to set history free from the futility of determination from the past.

THE PARABLES AS INVITATIONS TO GOD'S REIGN

The problem that confronts us is how we may ourselves appropriate the power of God's Reign. We have granted throughout this study that the Reign of God that Jesus announces and embodies is not a plain fact that hits the disinterested observer "between the eyes." It is an announcement that requires not so much assent as participation. We have to participate in and rely upon its power in order to comprehend its meaning. No wonder Jesus said that to those outside it was like a riddle (Mark 4:11)![21]

The parables represent an invitation to interpret possibilities for this world through the realities glimpsed in the parables. It is this world, and not another, which is even now transfused with the decisive action of God announced in Jesus Christ. As the church was later to confess, it is this life, here and now, that is set free from futility by the death and resurrection of Jesus Christ. To repent and believe in God's Reign, therefore, is to entertain and rely upon an alternative view of the future and to see in it the working out of God's purposes.

In one parable after another, the behavior that is commended is that in which an individual grasps the potential of a future development and acts decisively in the present to prepare for it. A discharged manager acts hurriedly to assure himself some livelihood when he is no longer employed. An errant son stakes his future on the mercy of a father. The parables invite the hearer to break out of the predictability of the present by living now in the light of the inbreaking Reign of God. To "enter the Kingdom" or to live in God's Reign now is to allow the realities glimpsed through the parables to form the context for our decisions now.

A classmate of mine who is white went to serve as chaplain and professor at a predominantly black college at the height of the civil rights movement. He refused to believe that the historic enmity between black and white people in the community surrounding the college was inevitable. He and his wife lived under a constant threat of death from whites who resented his stand. Student volunteers stationed themselves around his house to protect him against the threats. In spite of their efforts, however, members of the white community tampered with the brakes on his car, and a planned "accident" injured him seriously, permanently scarring his face.

He steadfastly refused to accept the notion that the future of that community had simply to be a replication of the tragic hate and racism of the past. He, along with friends and co-workers, had an alternative vision. When he spoke of his commitments to that community, he said, "My wife and I are committed to racial justice. We may never live to see an integrated society in this community, so we've decided to enjoy it now." He lived in an alternative future.

> These all died in faith, not having received what was promised, but having seen it and greeted it from afar, and having acknowledged that they were strangers and exiles on the earth. For people who speak thus make it clear that they are seeking a homeland. If they had been thinking of that land from which they had gone out, they would have had opportunity to return. But as it is, they desire a better country, that is, a heavenly one. Therefore, God is not ashamed to be called their God, for he has prepared for them a city. (Heb. 11:13–16)

Implicit in the word "glimpses" is the notion that the view of God's Reign that we find in the parables is partial and fleeting. It is sufficient to acquaint us with major outlines and shapes of God's Reign, but there is never sufficient information to satisfy our curiosity. We are given enough to win our loyalty to it but never enough information to satisfy the questions we bring. The parables are not intended to satisfy our curiosity but to present us with a world whose very attractiveness and credibility will win our devotion.

Reacting to the parables is a participative undertaking. Discovering the power of God's Reign is much like becoming acquainted with the buoyancy of water. We experience it when we come to rely upon it, when we entrust ourselves to it. We show that we have "gotten the point" of the parables when we come to rely upon the force of grace and novelty that they disclose.

A natural response to a serious study of a parable, therefore, is to ask what sort of action the parable suggests in your situation. Parables sometimes end with the suggestion that a certain action is fitting or logically necessary (see Luke 15:32).

The power of God's Reign, like the buoyancy of water, is

apparent only to those who yield themselves to it. The parables, therefore, are depictions of the power that is present in our situation. They are invitations to trust in this power by acting out tangible signs of the hope that is ours.

The Church as Parable of God's Reign

The church by its nature is a representative and anticipative fellowship that relies upon the power of God's Reign. However far the human body of the church falls short of this ideal, its vocation in history is to be a body of visionaries, a community of pioneers, who have glimpsed the future in Christ and who struggle to embody that future by tangible actions here and now.

The future to which the church bears witness is not a closed circle; it is the future for all people. As a representative body, the church acts on behalf of the whole human race in heeding the promise of God's Reign and in giving it perceptible form now. In its representative function the church is always "a preliminary taking possession of what is to come for other people and other things."[22]

The church lives in the time in which God's Reign has been glimpsed in Christ, and yet it waits for the time of its full appearing. Living as it does between the first appearance and the full dawning of God's Reign, the task of the church is to invest itself in undertakings that exhibit marks of God's Reign. "Wherever a community of faith responds to the action of God in Christ by exhibiting here and now tangible and perceptible signs of his coming kingdom of love and righteousness and peace, there you have a true body of Christ entitled to be called the church."[23]

The church, in short, is to be a parable of God's Reign. It is to offer a glimpse, a momentary apprehension, of the manner in which the Reign of God appears in human affairs. When it joins in action with the poor and dispossessed, those alienated and alone, it not only offers assistance but makes a declaration about the coming Reign of God. When it stands by the side of those who, by most estimates, are "nobodies," it provides a glimpse of their standing in God's Reign. When it puts resources into the hands of those who have been denied them, it bears witness to the drastic reversal of God's Reign. The church, in short, declares by speech and by action that those formerly thought to be of little consequence, those thought reprehensible and suspect, are first in the Reign of God and first, therefore, in the focus of the church as well.

None of this is to suggest that the outreach of the church is merely an illustrated sermon. It is not to imply that ministries are offered only as media for providing signals of God's Reign. It is, however, to contend that the church's proclamation of God's mighty acts in Jesus Christ and the church's action by the side of the dispossessed are fundamentally one and are not to be separated.

Worship and outreach are both glimpses of God's Reign. In our worship we tell and re-tell those stories that keep alive in our imagination and vision the reality of God's Reign when it appears. We are a story-telling people. We customarily answer the question of who we are by answering the prior question of what story we are a part of.[24] The stories that give us our identity as a church begin with Creation and end with those intimations of last things when God's purpose prevails for all.

The sacraments, then, become parables reminding us that all of reality can be the bearer of God's presence. At baptism we induct new members into the body of hope. At the Lord's Table we "act out" the future. For in the midst of hunger, flat up against the reality of the exclusion of vast portions of the human race at the table of life, the church leaps ahead in time when those who are now hungry and excluded will stream to the Table. And in place of starvation and greed, oppression and humiliation, all will own one another as sister and brother; all will acknowledge that each belongs. When we gather at the Lord's Table, we "act out" this future.

Our boldest actions as the church are only provisional signs, anticipatory tokens, of God's Reign. Never do they embody it adequately. This is not to excuse ourselves from responsible action while God's children perish. But it is to confess that the logic of the church's action in history is not exhausted by the odds on its success.

We quoted Alfred North Whitehead's definition of religion at the beginning of this study. In the light of the parables, it is worth hearing once again. Religion "is the vision of something that stands beyond, behind, and within, the passing flux of immediate things, something that is real, and yet waiting to be realized, something that is a remote possibility and yet the greatest of present facts, something whose possession is the final good, and yet is beyond reach: something that is the ultimate ideal and the hopeless quest."[25] These words would serve as well in describing God's Reign. It has dawned in Christ. Its final appearance is yet before us. In the meantime, it is the most basic of the realities with which we have to deal; and yet it is beyond our grasp. We see it in glimpses and provisional signs. Let the one with eyes to see prepare to use them now!

QUESTIONS AND SUGGESTED METHODS

1. By what signs or symbols do you recognize anticipations of God's Reign in your own life and in your community? At what moments have you witnessed signs of the Reign of God?

2. Jesus used parables as fleeting expressions of the force of God's Reign when it appeared. Can you compose a parable for the present day that would help someone who knew nothing of God's Reign experience it? Who are the characters, the setting, the action? Share your parables with one another.

3. People in the parables who were confronted with the Reign of God frequently had some investment in the old age that prevented their joining in the joy and demands of the new (see, for example, the elder brother or the Pharisee praying in the Temple). What are the barriers within you as an individual that blind you to seeing God's Reign when it appears or from heeding it when it is seen? What would you need to lose if you joined God's Reign? What would you gain?

4. Does a vision of God's Reign make you more satisfied or less satisfied with situations that contradict or mock God's Reign? What does the answer reveal about your vision? Does the vision of God's Reign in the parables give you more hope or less hope for dealing with the injustice in present structures?

5. Throughout this study we have spoken of the presence of God's Reign in the midst of the old age. Select symbols of the old age and the new and portray their interaction on a poster, banner, slide transparency, or videotape. What are the primary symbols of the old and the new?

6. Jesus called hypocrites those who were proficient in day-to-day technical information sufficient to manage their immediate affairs and yet who had little understanding of the nature of the times in which they were living (Luke 12:54–56). He suggested that only those who were alive to what God was doing in their history would heed the call to God's Reign. Make two parallel columns. In the first column list three concerns that you have for your community, three concerns for the nation, and three concerns for the world. In the second column, note significant ties, if you find them, to what you have learned of God's Reign through the study of the parables. Is there anything about the relationship or lack of it that is surprising to you? What intentions about your own concerns and ministries occur to you as a result of this analysis?

Notes

1. Robert Heilbroner, *An Inquiry into the Human Prospect* (New York: W. W. Norton, 1974), pp. 136–138.

2. Ibid., p. 138.

3. Willis W. Harman, "Planning Amid Forces for Institutional Change" (A presentation at the symposium "Planning in the Seventies," co-sponsored by the Washington Chapter of the American Society for Public Administration and the National Bureau of Standards on May 3–4, 1971). See also his *An Incomplete Guide to the Future* (San Francisco: San Francisco Book Company, 1976) and his "Notes on the Coming Transformation," in *The Next 25 Years*, ed. Andrew A. Spekke (Washington: World Future Society, 1975), pp. 10–22.

4. Marilyn Ferguson, *The Aquarian Conspiracy: Personal and Social Transformation in the 1980s* (New York: St. Martin's Press, [1980] 1987).

5. Ibid., p. 51.

6. Ibid., pp. 30, 42.

7. Ibid., pp. 66, 90.

8. Ibid., pp. 42.

9. Ibid., p. 19.

10. Ibid., p. 37.

11. Ibid., pp. 42, 43.

12. Ibid., p. 70.

13. Reminding one of Martin Luther's definition of God: "Faith of the heart alone make both God and an idol.... For the two, faith and

God, have inevitable connection. Now, I say whatever your heart clings to and confides in, that is really your God" (*Luther's Large Catechism*, trans. J. N. Lenker [Minneapolis: Augsburg Publishing House, 1967], p. 10).

14. Jürgen Moltmann, *Religion, Revolution and the Future*, trans. M. Douglas Meeks (New York: Charles Scribner's Sons, 1969), pp. 195ff.

15. The point was not missed by *Newsweek* several years ago in its commentary on the release of a new Superman movie. *Newsweek* acknowledged that the film cast Superman as "son of God, as the Saviour, as the Resurrection and the Life" and concludes: "Films like 'Close Encounters of the Third Kind,' 'Superman' and even 'Star Wars' have become jerry-built substitutes for the great myths and rituals of belief, hope and redemption that cultures used to shape before mass secular society took over" (Jack Kroll, "Superman to the Rescue," *Newsweek* 43:1 [January 1, 1979], p. 50).

16. These and other expressions of salvation stories were suggested by Robert Jewett and are discussed in the volume that he co-authored with John S. Lawrence, *The American Monomyth* (New York: Doubleday, 1977). See also Jewett's *The Captain American Complex: The Dilemma of Zealous Nationalism*, rev. ed. (Santa Fe: Bear & Co., 1984).

17. Robert Coles, "The Cold, Tough World of the Affluent Family," *Psychology Today* 9:6 (November 1975), p. 68.

18. Robert Bundy ed., *Images of the Future* (Buffalo: Prometheus Books, 1976), p. 2.

19. Richard Shaull, "The Death and Resurrection of the American Dream," in Gustavo Gutiérrez and Richard Shaull, *Liberation and Change* (Atlanta: John Knox, 1977), p. 120.

20. Paulo Freire, *Pedagogy of the Oppressed*, trans. Myra Bergman Ramos (New York: Herder and Herder, 1972), p. 34.

21. The word for "parable" sometimes referred to a Hebrew Bible usage meaning "proverb" or "riddle." It is apparently this meaning that is implied in Mark 4:11.

22. Jürgen Moltmann, *The Church in the Power of the Spirit*, trans. Margaret Kohl (New York: Harper & Row, 1977), p. 195.

23. Alvin C. Porteus, *The Search for Christian Credibility* (New York: Abingdon, 1971), p. 181.

24. From a lecture by Alasdair MacIntyre, Boston University, March 29, 1978.

25. Alfred North Whitehead, *Science and the Modern World*, p. 228 (1933 ed.); quoted in Ian T. Ramsey, *Christian Discourse* (London: Oxford University, 1965), p. 66.

Appendix

Types of Parables
in the Synoptic Gospels

The term "parable" in the Synoptic Gospels refers to several types of figurative speech: The similitude, the parable proper, the illustration, and the allegory.[1] While all four forms are treated together in the foregoing discussion, the following paragraphs seek to distinguish them from one another.

The *similitude* recounts a "typical condition or a typical, recurrent event...."[2] The *parable proper*, on the other hand, tells of a particular situation of special interest.[3] The *similitude* simply refers to the pattern by which things work. It suggests, for example, what happens when leaven is added to meal (Matt. 13:33) or when we sow a mustard seed (Matt. 13:31ff.). Anyone on finding a lost sheep or a lost coin would rejoice (Luke 15:4–10). All these are similitudes in that they point to regular, predictable occurrences.

The *parable proper*, by contrast, refers not to what always happens but to a freely composed story relating something that *once happened*. It is what one person has done once.[4] Consequently, it recounts the story of a man who had a manager or a steward (Luke 16:1), a man who had two sons (Matt. 21:28), or a man who gave a great banquet (Luke 14:16). The *similitude* guards against objections from the audience by generalizing on typical happenings. The *parable proper* seeks to relate sometimes extraordinary events in such a convincing fashion that opposition is hushed by the believability and winsomeness of the story itself.[5]

The *illustration* is to be distinguished from both the similitude and the parable proper. The parable proper draws some correspondence between two realities. The illustration, on the other hand, simply produces an example. The Parable of the Good Samaritan produces an illustration of one who proves to be a neighbor to a man who is beaten and robbed, as well as illustrations of those who were not neighbors (Luke 10:26–37). The Parable of the Publican and the Pharisee (Luke 18:1–8) likewise produces illustrations of conduct that is exemplary. A parable proper cites an occurrence on one level and compares it to another. For example, the crafty, wily preparation of the unjust steward (Luke 16:1–8) is commended as a comparison for the diligence and single-mindedness that should be directed toward entering the Reign of God. The illustration, by contrast, does not involve a comparison on more than one level. It simply produces examples of behavior or attitudes that are instructive in themselves.

The *allegory*, in distinction to the three types we have discussed, uses several elements of the story to refer to something quite removed from the story.[6] Whereas the parable proper will usually have one major point, "one central focus,"[7] the allegory may have several references. For example, in the Parable of the Sower (Mark 4:3–8 and par.), the seed that is sown is the Word; the birds that devour it represent Satan. The seeds that fell on rocky ground represent those who at first believed and then succumbed in the time of tribulation. Each element of the allegory stands for something else. The story serves only as a cue so that its individual parts can serve as code references to the message within the message.

The allegory is spoken or written for the one who is an "insider." Comprehension of its meaning depends upon knowing the code, understanding what each element in the story *really* represents. Unless the code is given people can speculate endlessly about the hidden meanings of the allegory.

The parable proper does not depend upon an encoded message. Its meaning should be utterly transparent. The parable proper is not aimed at those who are "insiders" but at ones whom the speaker is seeking to convince. "The parable speaks... to opponents, the allegory to the initiated. The parable is used to reconcile opposition, the allegory presupposes an understanding."[8]

Throughout most of the history of the Christian church, the parables have been interpreted as allegories.[9] Each parable has presented a rich repository of messages to the devoted imagination. Origen of Alexandria (185–254), for example, suggested that in the Parable of the Good Samaritan the man who fell among thieves was Adam. Jerusalem represented heaven, and Jericho stood for the world. The priest and the Levites signified the Law and the prophets. The beast that bore the wounded traveler stood for the body of Christ that bore the wounded Adam. The inn in the parable represents the church. The two pence signify the Father and the Son, and the Samaritan's promise to return again points to Christ's Second Coming.[10]

Most recent students of the parables, however, have regarded few of Jesus' parables as allegories. Particularly since the work of the German scholar Adolf Julicher in 1888, the tendency for most persons studying the parables has been to regard them not as repositories of secret messages but as straightforward stories seeking to make a single point. This point, in most cases, is a response to critics and is thus rooted in an incident in Jesus' ministry.

Sensitivity to the various types of sayings that are grouped together in the New Testament as parables can help us to interpret the parables more faithfully. They need to be understood within the context of Jesus' ministry and within the framework of his teachings as a whole. They need to be interpreted, for the most part, not as encoded messages whose meanings would be intelligible only to the "insiders." Jesus used them to announce God's Reign and to welcome his hearers to respond in faith and to experience that New Age as a present reality.

Notes

1. Eta Linnemann, *Jesus of the Parables*, trans. John Sturdy (New York: Harper & Row, 1964), pp. 3ff.
2. Rudolf Bultmann, *The History of the Synoptic Tradition*, trans. John Marsh (New York: Harper & Row, 1963), p. 174.
3. Ibid.
4. Linnemann, *Jesus of the Parables*, p. 4.
5. Ibid.
6. There is a significant and useful distinction to be made, we believe, between an allegory and the "parable proper," as we have termed it here. It should be noted that not all would accept such a distinction. Boucher stresses the need to understand parables as two interrelated types of indirect (vs. literal) meaning. Boucher understands allegory as a much wider category than we have acknowledged here, and she particularly denies that an allegory must be a series of metaphors. On the contrary, it may be shaped not by a variety of metaphors but reflect metaphorical meaning as a totality. Thus she concludes, unlike the definitions given here: "Any parable which has both a literal and a metaphorical meaning is an allegory" (Madeleine Boucher, *The Mysterious Parable* [Washington: Catholic Biblical Association of America, 1977], p. 21; see also pp. 11–25).
7. The phrase used by John Donahue, (*The Gospel in Parable* (Philadelphia: Fortress Press, 1988), p. 12.
8. Linnemann, *Jesus of the Parables*, p. 7.
9. Archibald Hunter, *Interpreting the Parables* (Philadelphia: Westminster, 1960), pp. 25–26.
10. There are notable exceptions to this view, to be sure. The most categorical disagreement with it is John Drury in the work cited at several points in this study, *The Parables in the Gospels: History and Allegory* (London: SPCK, 1985). Drury considers it impossible to reach any solid conclusion about the authenticity of the parables as creations of Jesus himself and believes that we must be content to study them in the light of first century Christianity and the overarching interest of the three synoptic evangelists (pp. 3–4).

Glossary

Allegory: A symbolic story in which details of the story stand for something else, usually general truths or generalizations about human experience. Interpretation of the allegory depends upon knowing the code by which the symbolic references are disclosed. Unlike the parable, the story need not be a typical or even a credible occurrence in order to convey its message.

Apocalyptic: The literature and the images and symbols developed out of the view that the present order, ruled over by the forces of wickedness, will be destroyed and replaced by the rule of God.

Apocalypticism: Means "uncovering." Highly symbolic writing referring to the time when God will destroy this wicked world and will initiate a new heavenly order.

Apocrypha: The name applied to the collection of books not included in the Jewish Bible but that were included in the Greek translation of it. The books were written between 200 B.C. and A.D. 100. In some editions of the English Bible, they appear between the Old and the New Testaments.

Christology: The understanding of the person and nature of Christ and Christ's relationship to God.

Eschatology: A teaching concerning "last things" and the end of history.

Essenes: A disciplined Jewish religious community in Palestine at the time of Jesus. As ones separated out from the rest of society they believed themselves to be the people of a New Covenant that under God would be established in the last days.

Evangelist: A word taken from the Greek word for the Gospel, or "good news." Used to refer to the one who proclaims the good news, or the author of one of the four Gospels.

Ezra Apocalypse: Chapters 3–14 or the Book of 2 Esdras, a book of the apocrypha. Series of apocalyptic visions addressing the problem of evil and the coming of the Messiah. Dates to approximately 100 A.D.

Kaddish: A prayer in the language that Jesus spoke, Aramaic, and one that was and still is a regular part of synagogue worship. Its title, meaning "sanctification," referred to the petition in the prayer, "Magnified and hallowed be His great name."

Law: The teaching of Yahweh revealed in the first five books of the Hebrew Bible. The term also was used more inclusively to mean the totality of God's self-revelation, written and oral.

Maccabean Wars: Revolts of the Jews against attempts of Syrian Greek rulers to impose heathen worship upon the Jews. The rebellion broke out in 167 B.C. when the priest Mattathias slew the king's representative. Under Mattathias's son, Judas Maccabeus, the rebellion controlled virtually all of Judea and restored the Temple (in 165 B.C.) from its former profanation.

Messianic Banquet: The joyous meal at which the Messiah is to be the host and the righteous of all the nations feast. The meal is mentioned in Isaiah 25:6 and forms the basis for Jesus' words to his disciples at the Last Supper (Matt. 26:29/Mark 14:25/Luke 22:18).

Metaphor: A phrase in which a word or words referring to one type of object are used in place of the normal words for quite a different kind of object, in order to suggest an analogy or parallel between the two. For example, references to people as "the salt of the earth," to a child as "the apple of my eye," or an impressive leader as a "tower of strength" are metaphors.

Midrash: The name for interpretations of Scripture made by rabbis in ancient Palestine. These interpretations sought to clarify the meaning of the Scriptures and establish guides for conduct from them.

Parable: A story involving metaphor, simile, and, sometimes, features of allegory told for the purpose of religious teaching. Usually a parable conveys one central point and is told in such fashion that the listener experiences a new insight through the comparison of two entities usually considered unlike. The story may be fictitious or an actual happening. Its effect depends upon its credibility as an event that could happen in common experience.

Paradigm: A basic model or picture of the physical order and its interrelationships, such as the model of the universe as a great machine.

Qumran: The site of an Essene monastery overlooking the Dead Sea.

Resurrection: This term refers to a variety of beliefs in the awakening of the dead and, in some cases, the resuscitation of their bodies after death. Resurrection was a belief held by Jesus and the Pharisees but not by the Sadducees.

Scribe: A group who were professional interpreters and teachers of the Law.

Simile: An expression comparing two things ordinarily considered unrelated. One thing is said to be *like* another.

Similitudes of Enoch: The Book of Enoch (dated about 94–79 B.C.) was a book of 108 chapters well known to Jesus' contemporaries and to the first Christians. Chapters 37–71 (Book 2) are known as the Similitudes, or Parables, and consist of stories concerning the final judgment of the wicked, the coming of the Son of Man, and the rewards that await the righteous.

Synagogue: An assembly of the Jewish community for the purpose of reading and study of the Scriptures and for prayer. The synagogue as an institution originated during the Exile in Babylonia when it was impossible for the faithful to worship in the Temple.

Synoptic Gospels: The first three Gospels. The word "synoptic" refers to the common point of view that they take of Jesus' ministry and teachings as distinguished from that of the fourth Gospel, John.

Talmud: An oral and later a written tradition of commentary on the Scriptures, seeking by story and commentary to instill knowledge of and obedience to God's teaching. The Talmud was formed during a period of about a thousand years, from the time of Ezra to the sixth century A.D.

Zealot: One who was a radical rebel against outside domination of Israel by Rome. Also, more widely, one who was a radically committed agent of Yahweh to combat idolatry and transgression of the Law.

Bibliography

Bailey, Kenneth E. *Poet and Peasant: A Literary Cultural Approach to the Parables in Luke.* Grand Rapids, Mich.: William B. Eerdmans Publishing Company, 1976.

————. *Through Peasant Eyes: More Lucan Parables, Their Culture and Style.* Grand Rapids, Mich.: William B. Eerdmans Publishing Company, 1980.

Bornkamm, Gunter. *Jesus of Nazareth.* Translated by Irene and Fraser McLuskey with James M. Robinson. New York: Harper & Row, Publishers, 1960.

Borsch, Frederick H. *Many Things in Parables.* Philadelphia: Fortress Press, 1988.

Boucher, Madeleine. *The Mysterious Parable: A Literary Study.* Washington: The Catholic Biblical Association of America, 1977.

Caird, G. B. *The Gospel of Luke.* Baltimore: Penguin Books, 1963.

Crossan, John Dominic. *Cliffs of Fall: Paradox and Polyvalence in the Parables of Jesus.* New York: The Seabury Press, 1980.

————. *Finding Is the First Act: Trove Folktales and Jesus' Treasure Parable.* Philadelphia: Fortress Press, 1979.

————. *In Parables: The Challenge of the Historical Jesus.* New York: Harper & Row, Publishers, 1973.

Derrett, J. Duncan. *Studies in the New Testament.* Vol. 1: *Glimpses of the Legal and Social Presuppositions of the Authors.* Leiden: E. J. Brill, 1977.

————. *Studies in the New Testament.* Vol. 3: *Midrash, Haggadah, and the Character of the Community.* Leiden: E. J. Brill, 1982.

Dodd, C. H. *The Parables of the Kingdom.* London: Nisbet & Co., Ltd. (1935) 1956.

Donahue, John R. *The Gospel in Parable: Metaphor, Narrative, and Theology in the Synoptic Gospels.* Philadelphia: Fortress Press, 1988.

Drury, John. *The Parables in the Gospels: History and Allegory.* London: SPCK, 1985.

Funk, Robert W. *Language, Hermeneutic, Word of God: The Problem of Language in the New Testament and Contemporary Theology.* New York: Harper & Row, Publishers, 1966.

Hunter, Archibald M. *Interpreting the Parables.* Philadelphia: Westminster Press, 1960.

Jeremias, Joachim. *Jerusalem in the Time of Jesus.* Translated by F. H. and C. H. Cave. Philadelphia: Fortress Press, 1969.

———. *The Parables of Jesus.* Translated by S. H. Hooke. 2nd revised edition. New York: Charles Scribner's Sons, 1972.

Kingsbury, Jack Dean. *The Parables of Jesus in Matthew 13: A Study in Redaction-Criticism.* Richmond, Virginia: John Knox Press, 1969.

Kissinger, Warren. *The Parables of Jesus: A History of Interpretation and Bibliography.* Metuchen, N.J.: Scarecrow Press, 1979.

Kee, Howard Clark. *Jesus in History: An Approach to the Study of the Gospels.* Rev. ed. New York: Harcourt Brace Jovanovich, 1977 (1970).

Kummel, Werner George. *Promise and Fulfillment: The Eschatological Message of Jesus.* Translated by Dorothea M. Barton. 3d rev. ed. London: SCM Press, (1957) 1969.

Ladd, George Eldon. *The Presence of the Future: The Eschatology of Biblical Realism.* Grand Rapids, Mich.: William B. Eerdmans Publishing Co., 1974.

Linnemann, Eta. *Jesus of the Parables.* Translated by John Study. New York: Harper & Row, Publishers, 1966.

Manson, T. W. *The Sayings of Jesus.* London: SCM Press, 1937, 1961.

———. *The Teaching of Jesus: Studies of Its Form and Content.* Cambridge: Cambridge University Press, 1955 (1931).

Nineham, D. E. *The Gospel of St. Mark.* Baltimore: Penguin Books. 1963.

Oesterley, W. O. E. *The Gospel Parables in the Light of Their Jewish Background.* London: Society for Promoting Christian Knowledge, 1936.

Perkins, Pheme. "Interpreting Parables: The Bible and the Humanities." In *Emerging Issues in Religious Education*, Gloria Durka and Joan-Marie Smith, eds., pp. 149–172. New York: Paulist Press, 1976.

Perrin, Norman. *Rediscovering the Teaching of Jesus.* New York: Harper & Row, Publishers, 1976 (1964).

Purdy, John C. *Parables at Work.* Philadelphia: Westminster Press, 1985.

Riesenfeld, Harald, "The Parables in the Synoptic and in the Johannine Traditions." In *The Gospel Tradition.* Chapter 7, pp. 139–169. Philadelphia: Fortress Press, 1970.

Sanford, John A. *The Kingdom Within: A Study of the Inner Meaning of Jesus' Sayings.* New York: J. B. Lippincott Company, 1970.

Snodgrass, Klyne. *The Parable of the Wicked Tenants: An Inquiry into Parable Interpretation.* Tubingen: J. C. B. Mohr, 1983.

Stein, Robert H. *An Introduction to the Parables of Jesus.* Philadelphia: Westminster Press, 1981.

———. *The Method and Message of Jesus' Teachings.* Philadelphia: Westminster Press, 1978.

TeSelle, Sallie McFague. *Speaking in Parables: A Study in Metaphor and Theology.* Philadelphia: Fortress Press, 1975.

Tolbert, Mary Ann. *Perspectives on the Parables: An Approach to Multiple Interpretations.* Philadelphia: Fortress Press, 1979.

Wilder, Amos N. *Early Christian Rhetoric.* Cambridge, Mass.: Harvard University Press, 1971.

PARABLES IN THE SYNOPTIC GOSPELS

		Matthew	Mark	Luke	Gospel Parallels	Pages in Text
1.	New Patches on Old Garments	9:16	2:21	5:36	54	50
2.	New Wine/New Wineskins	9:17	2:22	5:37–39	54	50
3.	The Sower	13:3–8	4:3–8	8:5–8	90	108
4.	The Seed Growing Secretly		4:26–29		90	113
5.	The Mustard Seed	13:31f	4:30–32	13:18f	164	114
6.	The Wicked Tenants	21:33–44	12:1–11	20:9–18	204	127
7.	The Fig Tree	24:32f	13:28f	21:29–31	220	47
8.	The Doorkeeper		13:33–37	12:35–38	222	44
9.	Going before the Judge	5:25f		12:58f	22	93
10.	The Two Houses	7:24–27		6:47–49	43	–
11.	Children in the Marketplace	11:16–19		7:31–35	65	23
12.	The Return of Evil Spirit	12:43–45		11:24–26	88	–
13.	The Weeds	13:24–30			96	114
14.	The Leaven	13:33		13:20f	98	115
15.	The Hidden Treasure	13:44			101	70
16.	The Pearl	13:45			101	70
17.	The Net	13:47f			102	125
18.	The Lost Sheep	18:12–14		15:4–7	133	58
19.	The Unmerciful Servant	18:23–25			136	100
20.	The Laborers in the Vineyard	20:1–16			190	86
21.	The Two Sons	21:28–32			203	80
22.	The Marriage Feast	22:1–10		14:16–24	205	98
23.	The Guest without a Wedding Garment	22:11–14			205	–
24.	The Burglar	24:43f		12:39f	225	47
25.	The Faithful and Wise Servant	24:45–51		12:42–46	226	45

		Matthew	Mark	Luke	*Gospel Parallels*	Pages in Text
26.	The Ten Maidens	25:1–13			227	48
27.	The Talents	25:14–30		19:12–27	228	124
28.	The Last Judgment	25:31–46			229	122
29.	The Two Debtors			7:41–43	83	29
30.	The Good Samaritan			10:25–37	144	83
31.	The Friend at Midnight			11:5–8	147	116
32.	The House and Kingdom Divided	12:25–26	3:23–26	11:17–20	149	40
33.	The Strong Man's House	12:29	3:27	11:21–22	150	40
34.	The Watchful Servants			12:42–48	158/159	45
35.	The Rich Fool			12:16–21	156	89
36.	The Barren Fig Tree			13:6–9	162	125
37.	The Closed Door			13:24–30	165	121
38.	The Choice Places at the Table			14:7–11	169	102
39.	The Tower-builder and the King Contemplating a Campaign			14:28–32	171	94
40.	The Lost Coin			15:8–10	172	61
41.	The Prodigal Son			15:11–32	173	63
42.	The Unjust Steward			16:1–8	174	95
43.	The Rich Man and Lazarus			16:19–31	177	81
44.	The Servant's Wages			17:7–10	181	102
45.	The Unjust Judge			18:1–8	185	118
46.	The Pharisee and the Publican			18:9–14	186	78

Note: Title for the parables and *Gospel Parallels* numbers are taken from Burton H. Throckmorton, Jr., ed., *Gospel Parallels* (New York: Thomas Nelson & Sons, 1957). The last column refers to pages in this text in which the parable is discussed.

Index of Scripture References

Exodus ——————
3:1, *60*
22:22, *132*

Leviticus ——————
11:10–12, *126*
25:23, *63*

Deuteronomy ——————
10:18, *132*
20:7, *99*
21:15–17, *63*
24:5, *99*

2 Samuel ——————
12:1–4, *22*
14:33, *67*

1 Kings ——————
19:20, *8*
20:35–40, *22*

2 Kings ——————
1:2, *41*
1:8, *10*

Psalms ——————
23:5, *98*
68:5, *132*
118, *129*
119:176, *73*

Isaiah ——————
1:17, *132*

5:1–5, *128*
5:1–7, *22*
6:9, *109*
6:9f., *109*
6:10, *109*
24:21–23, *10*
25:6, *162*
25:6–9, *98*
33:22, *10*
40:11, *60*
42:1, *40*
49:22, *60*
53:6, *73*

Jeremiah ——————
22:3, *132*

Ezekiel ——————
19:2–9, *22*
34:17, *122*

Daniel ——————
7:13, *9*

Joel ——————
3:13, *113*

Micah ——————
2:12ff., *10*
4:1–7, *10*

Zephaniah ——————
3:14–20, *10*

Matthew ——————
3:17, *128*
4:17b, *7*
5:20–48, *7*
5:25–26, *93*
9:15, *48*
9:16, *50*
9:17, *50*
10:23, *39, 52*
11:19, *58*
12:1–2, *41*
12:9–14, *41*
12:22–23, *41*
12:24, *41*
12:25–29, *40*
12:27, *41*
12:29, *145*
12:32, *13*
12:40, *52*
13:3–8, *108*
13:10–15, *111*
13:11–14, *109*
13:13, *77*
13:14–15, *131*
13:18–23, *110*
13:22, *13*
13:24–30, *114*
13:31–32, *114*
13:31ff., *157*
13:32, *115*
13:33, *115, 157*
13:36–43, *110*
13:41, *52*
13:44, *26*
13:44–46, *70*
13:45, *26*
13:47–50, *125*
16:16, *40*
16:27, *122*
17:5, *128*
18:12–14, *25, 36, 58*
18:24–35, *100*
18:27, *101*

18:28, *42, 101*
19:5, *65*
19:28, *40, 52*
20:1–16, *86*
20:4, *86*
20:15, *87*
20:33–41, *106*
21:23ff., *80*
21:28, *157*
21:28–32, *29, 80*
21:31, *25*
21:31–32, *57*
21:33–44, *127*
21:34, *127*
21:39, *128*
21:45, *128*
21:45f., *129*
22:1–10, *78, 98*
22:7, *98, 99*
22:10, *98*
22:23–40, *27*
22:34–35, *83*
23, *27*
23:2, *28*
23:12, *103*
23:13–15, *28*
23:34–36, *48*
24:27, *52*
24:32f., *47*
24:33, *48*
24:37, *52*
24:38–39, *47*
24:39, *40, 52*
24:42–44, *47*
24:44, *52*
24:45, *46*
24:45–51, *45, 66*
24:47, *46*
25:1–13, *48*
25:12, *50*
25:14–15b, *44*
25:14–30, *65, 124*
25:25, *71*

25:31, *40, 52, 122*
25:31–46, *122*
25:34, *123*
25:40, *123*
26:29, *162*

Mark ——————————
1:6, *10*
1:11, *128*
1:15, *7, 8, 93, 139*
1:16–20, *7*
1:17, *93*
1:22, *12, 21*
1:24, *12*
2:11, *149*
2:19, *48*
2:21, *50*
3:22, *41, 50*
3:23–27, *40*
3:27, *145*
4:3–8, *108, 158*
4:9, *131*
4:10–12, *111*
4:11, *111, 150, 156*
4:11–12, *109*
4:11f., *14*
4:12, *109, 111*
4:13–20, *110*
4:26, *113*
4:26–29, *112, 113*
4:27, *112*
4:28, *112, 113*
4:29, *113*
4:30–32, *114*
4:31, *115*
4:32, *115*
4:34, *21*
6:46, *94*
8:28, *10*
8:29, *111*
8:29–31, *40*
8:38, *52, 122*
9:7, *128*

9:9, *52*
9:11, *10*
12:1–12, *127*
12:2, *127*
12:6, *128*
12:7, *127*
12:8, *128*
12:9a, *127*
12:12, *111, 128, 129*
12:28, *83*
13:14, *26, 43*
13:26, *52*
13:28f., *47*
13:29, *48*
13:30–32, *48*
13:33–37, *44*
13:34, *44*
14:25, *162*
15:35, *10*
15:41, *57*

Luke ——————————
1:70, *13*
2:25, *11, 142*
3:22, *128*
4:29, *7*
5:17, *27*
5:34, *48*
5:36–39, *50*
7:19, *142*
7:36–50, *57*
7:36–59, *101*
7:36ff., *27*
7:41–43, *29*
8:5–8, *108*
8:9–10, *111*
8:10, *109*
8:11–15, *110*
8:21, *57*
9:5, *8*
9:20, *40*
9:26, *122*
9:35, *128*

Luke (cont.) ———————
9:52–53, *85*
9:60, *8*
9:61, *94*
9:61–62, *8*
10:4, *8*
10:18, *14, 39*
10:25–37, *83*
10:26–37, *158*
10:33, *84*
10:36, *25*
10:37, *86*
10:38–42, *62*
11:5, *117*
11:5–8, *116*
11:8, *117, 118, 132*
11:14, *41*
11:15, *41*
11:17–23, *40*
11:19, *41*
11:20, *42*
11:21, *145*
11:22, *145*
11:30, *52*
12:13–21, *89*
12:19, *89*
12:20, *89*
12:35, *45*
12:35–38, *44*
12:37, *44, 45*
12:39–40, *47*
12:40, *52*
12:41, *45*
12:42, *46, 95*
12:42–46, *45, 66*
12:44, *46*
12:54–56, *8, 155*
12:57–59, *93*
13:1, *126*
13:4, *126*
13:6–9, *125*
13:18–19, *114*
13:19, *115*

13:20–21, *115*
13:24–30, *121*
13:26, *121, 122*
13:27, *121*
13:30, *122*
13:31, *27*
14:1, *27, 102*
14:7, *102*
14:7–11, *102*
14:11, *103*
14:15, *100*
14:16, *157*
14:16–24, *98*
14:18–20, *99*
14:21, *98, 100*
14:28–30, *94*
14:28–32, *94*
14:33, *94*
15:1–2, *55*
15:4, *59, 60*
15:4–7, *25, 36, 58*
15:4–10, *157*
15:6, *60*
15:7, *61*
15:8, *61, 62*
15:8–10, *61*
15:9, *62*
15:11, *63*
15:11–32, *25, 26, 63, 78*
15:12, *63*
15:13, *63, 95*
15:15, *65*
15:16, *66*
15:17, *66*
15:18–19, *66*
15:20, *67, 69*
15:21, *68*
15:22–24, *68*
15:26, *68*
15:28, *69*
15:29, *69*
15:30, *65*
15:31, *65, 69*

15:32, *69, 151*
16:1, *157*
16:1–8, *95, 158*
16:3, *95*
16:4, *96*
16:8, *97*
16:19–31, *81*
16:24, *82*
16:31, *82*
17:7–10, *104*
17:10, *104*
17:20, *27*
17:24, *52*
17:26, *52*
17:27, *47*
17:28–29, *47*
17:30, *40, 52*
18:1–8, *25, 56, 118, 158*
18:3, *119*
18:5, *119*
18:7, *119*
18:8, *40, 52, 120*
18:9–14, *15, 24, 78*
18:11, *57*
18:12, *80*
18:13, *80*
18:14, *103*
19:1–10, *58*
19:12–13, *44*
19:12–27, *124*
19:27, *125*
20:9–18, *127*
20:10, *127*
20:13, *128*
20:15, *129*
20:18, *129*
20:19, *128*
21:6, *48*
21:29–31, *47*

21:31, *48*
21:32–33, *48*
22:18, *162*
24:24, *100*

John ——————
4:9, *85*
4:13–15, *21*
5:8, *149*
6:35–41, *21*
8:13–18, *21*
8:48, *85*
9:2ff., *16*
9:16, *27*
10:7–18, *21*
11:28, *27*

Acts ——————
18:18, *21, 94*
23:6, *28*

2 Corinthians ——————
2:13, *94*
11:2, *49*

Philippians ——————
3:5, *28*

1 Thessalonians ——————
5:2, *53*

Hebrews ——————
2:14, *146*
2:15, *146*
11:13–16, *151*

James ——————
1:5–8, *118*

Index of Authors

Bailey, Kenneth Ewing, 73, 74,
    75, 84, 92, 106, 132
Barbour, Ian G., 36
Bell, Daniel, 36
Benz, Ernst, 19
Bornkamm, Gunther, 19, 35,
    73, 74
Borsch, Frederick H., 36, 106
Boucher, Madeleine, 111, 131,
    160
Broughton, James, 54
Bultmann, Rudolf, 19, 160
Bun bar Hijja, Rabbi, 88
Bundy, Robert, 156

Caird, G.B., 53, 69, 75, 132
Carlston, Charles E., 53
Coles, Robert, 143, 156
Crossan, John Dominic, 3, 34,
    36, 53, 75, 106
Cullmann, Oscar, 4, 19

Derrett, J. Duncan M., 73, 106,
    118, 132
Dodd, C.H., 23, 24, 35, 53,
    131, 133
Donahue, John, 133, 160
Drury, John, 35, 92, 106, 131,
    133, 160

Einstein, Albert, 30

Ferguson, Marilyn, 19, 139,
    140, 155

Fitzmyer, Joseph, 74, 132
Freire, Paulo, 156
Funk, Robert W., 35, 106

Gilmour, W. MacLean, 74, 106
Gould, Ezra P., 131

Harman, Willis, 139, 155
Heilbroner, Robert, 138, 155
Hillel, 78
Hunter, Archibald, 34, 53, 131,
    160

Jeremias, Joachim, 34, 35, 53,
    54, 73, 74, 92, 106, 131, 132,
    133
Jewett, Robert, 156
Johnson, Sherman E., 132
Jones, Geraint V., 92
Julicher, Adolf, 131, 159

Kee, Howard Clark, 19, 52
Kingsbury, Jack Dean, 131
Kissinger, Warren S., 132
Klausner, Joseph, 34
Kuhn, Thomas, 30, 36

Lawrence, John S., 156
Linnemann, Eta, 34, 35, 73, 74,
    92, 106, 131, 160

MacIntyre, Alasdair, 156
Manson, T. W., 34, 53, 92, 109,
    131, 132, 133

McFague TeSelle, Sallie, 35
Mead, Margaret, 1, 4
Moltmann, Jürgen, 156
Montefiore, C. G., 73
Mowry, Lucetta, 35

Nechunya b. Ha Kana, Rabbi,
92
Nineham, D.E., 19, 52, 53, 73

Oesterley, W.O.E., 34, 35, 54,
73, 74, 132, 133
Origen, 159

Perrin, Norman, 19, 35, 73,
132, 133
Plummer, Alfred, 53
Porteus, Alvin C., 156

Ramsey, Ian T., 4, 156
Richardson, Alan, 19, 52
Rivkin, Ellis, 35

Sanford, John, 132
Schnackenburg, R., 19
Shaull, Richard, 156
Snodgrass, Klyne, 133
Stein, Robert H., 73, 74, 131,
133
Stevens, Wallace, 140

Throckmorton, Jr., Burton H., 4

Via, Jr., Dan Otto, 92
Vincent, John J., 35

Whitehead, Alfred North, 2,
153, 156
Wilder, Amos, 21, 34, 35